NEW VANGUARD • 185

LAV-25

The Marine Corps' Light Armored Vehicle

JAMES D'ANGINA   ILLUSTRATED BY HENRY MORSHEAD

First published in Great Britain in 2011 by Osprey Publishing
PO Box 883, Oxford, OX1 9PL, UK
1385 Broadway, 5th Floor, New York, NY 10018, USA
Email: info@ospreypublishing.com

OSPREY is a trademark of Osprey Publishing, a division of Bloomsbury Publishing Plc

© 2011 Osprey Publishing

All rights reserved. Apart from any fair dealing for the purpose of private study, research, criticism or review, as permitted under the Copyright, Designs and Patents Act, 1988, no part of this publication may be reproduced, stored in a retrieval system, or transmitted in any form or by any means, electronic, electrical, chemical, mechanical, optical, photocopying, recording or otherwise, without the prior written permission of the copyright owner. Enquiries should be addressed to the Publishers.

Transferred to digital print on demand 2018.

First published 2011
2nd impression 2012

Printed and bound by PrintOnDemand-Worldwide.com, Peterborough, UK.

A CIP catalogue record for this book is available from the British Library.

Print ISBN: 978 1 84908 611 0
PDF eBook ISBN: 978 1 84908 612 7
ePub ISBN: 978 1 84908 903 6

Page layout by Melissa Orrom Swan, Oxford
Index by Alan Thatcher
Typeset in Sabon and Myriad Pro
Originated by United Graphics Pte Ltd

Artist's note
Readers may care to note that the original paintings and the 3D models from which the color plates in this book were prepared are available for private sale. All reproduction copyright whatsoever is retained by the Publishers. All inquiries should be addressed to:

hmxdesign@tiscali.co.uk

The Publishers regret that they can enter into no correspondence upon this matter.

The Woodland Trust
Osprey Publishing is supporting the Woodland Trust, the UK's leading woodland conservation charity, by funding the dedication of trees.

www.ospreypublishing.com

Glossary

AAV – Amphibious Assault Vehicle
AFV – armored fighting vehicle
APC – armored personnel carrier
APFSDS-T – Armor-Piercing Fin-Stabilized Discarding-Sabot Tracer
BLT – Battalion Landing Team
CCA – Composite Ceramic Armor system
CO – commanding officer
DMO – Defence Material Organisation
DOD – Department of Defense
EW – electronic warfare
FACT – Field Analysis Concepts Test
FAST – Fleet Anti-terrorist Security Team
FMS – Foreign Military Sales
FOB – Forward Operating Base
GCE – ground combat element
HEP – High-Explosive Plastic
HMMWV – High-Mobility Multipurpose Wheeled Vehicle
HUD – heads-up display
IED – improvised explosive device
IFV – infantry fighting vehicle
ITS – Infantry Training School
ITSS – Improved Thermal Sight System
LAI – Light Armored Infantry
LAR – Light Armored Reconnaissance
LAST – Light Appliqué System Technique
LAV – Light Armored Vehicle
LAV-AD – LAV Air Defense variant
LAV-AG – LAV Assault Gun variant
LAV-AT – LAV Antitank variant
LAV-C2 – LAV Command & Control variant
LAV-L – LAV Logistics variant
LAV-M – LAV Mortar variant
LAV-R – LAV Recovery variant
LCAC – Landing Craft, Air Cushion
MARFORP – Marine Forces Panama
MAW – Marine Air Wing
MEB – Marine Expeditionary Brigade
MEF – Marine Expeditionary Force
MEU – Marine Expeditionary Unit
MEWSS – Mobile Electronic Warfare System
MOS – Military Occupational Specialty
MPS – Maritime Prepositioning Ship
MSARC – Marine Corps Systems Review Council
OMLP – Operational Mentoring and Liaison Program
PDF – Panamanian Defense Forces
RCT – Regimental Combat Team
RDTF – Rapid Deployment Task Force
SANG – Saudi Arabian National Guard
SLEP – Service Life Extension Program
SOC – Special Operations Capable
SPMAGTF – Special Purpose Marine Air-Ground Task Force
TOW – Tube-launched, Optically Tracked, Wire command-link guided missile
TP-T – Target-Practice Tracer
ULC – Utility Landing Craft
UN – United Nations
UNITAF – Unified Task Force
XO – executive officer

CONTENTS

ORIGINS AND DEVELOPMENT 4
- Changes within the Corps

THE LAV-25 8
- Armament
- Marine Corps Variants
- Upgrades

OPERATIONS 23
- Panama
- Operation *Just Cause*
- Operation *Desert Shield/Storm*
- Operation *Uphold Democracy*
- Peace Enforcers
- Operation *Restore Hope*
- Operation *Joint Guardian*
- Operation *Enduring Freedom*
- Operation *Iraqi Freedom*

CONCLUSION 46

BIBLIOGRAPHY 46

INDEX 48

LAV-25
THE MARINE CORPS' LIGHT ARMORED VEHICLE

ORIGINS AND DEVELOPMENT

The United States' Light Armored Vehicle (LAV) Program began during the late 1970s. In response to escalating tensions in the Middle East, the Carter administration created the Rapid Deployment Force (RDF), following which a Rapid Deployment Task Force (RDTF) was formed. The RDTF established a requirement for an LAV to be used by rapid-deployment oriented units within the Department of Defense (DoD). In early 1980, the Senate Armed Services Committee approached the US Army and US Marine Corps about acquiring an "off the shelf" LAV. Both Army and Marine Corps leadership showed interest, and in April of 1981 proposal submissions were opened to 20 companies.

Three companies were selected for the final evaluation: Alvis Ltd of England, Cadillac Gage USA, and the Diesel Division of General Motors of Canada. Each company was required to provide three test vehicles, two utilizing the M242 Bushmaster 25mm chain gun and a single test bed incorporating a 90mm Cockerill cannon. Alvis Ltd submitted a Cockerill cannon mounted on the Scorpion 90 and three Stormer armored personnel carriers (APCs) armed with the M242 Bushmaster. The US Cadillac Gage company submitted two separate entries, the V-300 – a new design utilizing a 6x6 wheeled configuration – as well as a second entry based on a stretched V-150 Commando (re-designated V-150S). The only 8x8 configuration

An LAV-25 wearing a distinctive four-pattern desert camouflage scheme moves down a road along the Delta area of the Marine Corps Air-Ground Combat Center, Twentynine Palms, 1982. (DoD)

A Canadian Cougar based on the six-wheeled version of the Swiss MOWAG Piranha demonstrates the ability to overcome obstacles during an exhibition for Marine Corps officials at Quantico, VA, May 1979. (DoD)

submitted was built by General Motors of Canada; the entry was based on the Swiss Motorwagenfabrik AG (MOWAG) Piranha series of vehicles. The Canadian company had been manufacturing 6x6 versions of the Swiss Piranha under license since 1977. The Marine Corps leased six of these vehicles (Cougars and Grizzlies) from the Canadian Army and borrowed an M113 APC from the US Army for a Field Analysis Concepts Test (FACT) in 1979 to study weapon system tactics.

Testing of the LAV candidates took place at Twentynine Palms, California, and Yuma, Arizona. The commander of the US Army Tank-Automotive Command, Major General O.C. Decker Jr., oversaw procurement for both services and was the source selection authority. The Army's decision was then referred to the Marine Corps Systems Review Council (MSARC) headed by the Assistant Commandant of the Marine Corps for his decision. The Army expected to procure more than 2,350 vehicles, while the Marine Corps aimed to buy 744 examples of the winning vehicle.

In September 1982, one year after the final candidates were selected, a winner was chosen – the General Motors of Canada (later General Dynamics Land Systems) 8x8 vehicle. The Army had two variants scheduled before substituting the High-Mobility Multipurpose Wheeled Vehicle (HMMWV; "Humvee") for one of their LAV programs. The Army designated their version of the LAV as the M1047. The vehicle was similar to what the Marine Corps designated the LAV-25, but was not intended to carry dismounted troops. Instead the troop compartment was designed for additional ammunition and stowage. The US Army withdrew from the program completely due to funding problems. The Marine Corps, however, continued and eventually obtained funding to procure six variants: LAV-25 purposed for the 25mm Bushmaster; LAV-AT (Antitank); LAV-L (Logistics); LAV-R (Recovery); LAV-M (Mortar); and LAV-C2 (Command & Control). The vehicles were purchased within Fiscal Years 1982–85, and at the end of the program 758 LAVs had been built for the Corps, 14 more than originally planned.

Changes within the Corps

The new LAVs brought both doctrine and organizational challenges to the Marine Corps. The LAV was not replacing a current weapon system within an existing force structure – all of the organizations and doctrine needed

A Marine Corps Sikorsky CH-53E Super Stallion transports an LAV-25 as an external load from an expeditionary airfield to the Lavic Lake training area, Twentynine Palms, December 1982. One of the Marine Corps' requirements for the LAV was that it weighs less than 16 tons in order for the vehicle to be externally lifted by helicopter. (DoD)

creating from scratch. Delays in the Air Defense variant and later the cancellation of the Assault Gun variant forced the Marine Corps continually to modify the organizational structure of their battalions.

Inherent with the force structure changes came organizational name changes. Initially the battalions were called LAV battalions (LAVBs). In October 1988, the designation changed to Light Armored Infantry (LAI) battalions. Finally, in 1994, the name changed once more to Light Armored Reconnaissance (LAR) battalions, better reflecting the mission of the units.

The Infantry Training School (ITS) at Camp Pendleton, California, was given the mission to establish an LAV school in 1982. ITS was responsible for the training of all LAV crewmen under the new 0313 Military Occupational Specialty (MOS). The classes grew from a basic LAV Crewman course, to adding the Staff Non-Commissioned Officer & Officer Course in 1994. The same year the school would establish itself as a training company. In 2003 the LAV Training Company became an independent formal school under the School of Infantry. Curricula included an entry-level LAV Crewman Course, a Leaders Course and an Evaluator Course.

Company A (Reinforced) received the Marine Corps' first LAVs. The company was activated at Twentynine Palms on July 11, 1983, and started receiving the first of their vehicles in April 1984. With ten officers and

 LAV-25 ON EXERCISE, 1987

A Marine LAV-25 seen during Joint Exercise *Cold Winter 87*, a NATO exercise, February 1, 1987. The turret is turned 180 degrees to face the aft end of the vehicle, and the M242 Bushmaster 25mm chain gun still has its protective cover placed over the barrel. The crew have added snow chains and a temporary coat of white paint to the NATO three-color camouflage scheme to better adapt the vehicle to its extreme environment. The vehicle displays the name "HI-BODY" on the right side of the turret. Cold weather gear, sleeping bags, rolled bed mats (known as ISO mats in the Marine Corps), and a shovel are stowed on top of the small bustle rack.

250 enlisted personnel, Company A was considerably larger than what was planned for future LAV companies. The Marine Corps would eventually activate a total of four LAV battalions. The first was 2nd LAV Battalion activated in May 1985 at Camp Lejeune, North Carolina. This was followed by the 1st LAV Battalion, Camp Pendleton, and later Company A (Reinforced) evolved into the 3rd LAV Battalion still stationed at Twentynine Palms. On September 23, 1987, the 4th LAV Battalion was activated as a reserve battalion at Camp Pendleton.

The battalions were traditionally structured, with six companies consisting of the following: four line companies, a headquarters company, and a weapons company. At the company level the structure broke down into a company headquarters (HQ) and three LAV platoons. The platoons were further broken down into sections. The company HQ typically consisted of an LAV-C2 for the executive officer (XO), two LAV-Ls for logistical support, one LAV-R vehicle for recovery and maintenance operations, and an LAV-25 for the company commander. The three LAV platoons typically had a total of 12 LAV-25s and would be reinforced with mortar and antitank assets by the battalions' weapons company when needed.

THE LAV-25

The LAV-25 utilizes a hull made of welded armor steel plates designed to take direct hits from 7.62mm rounds and to protect the crew from artillery round fragments. The hull's exterior is covered with an anti-skid surface to enable the crew to walk safely on the vehicle's surface.

Power comes from a Detroit Diesel Allison turbocharged 6V53T (V-6) liquid-cooled two-stroke diesel engine producing 275hp, with an automatic

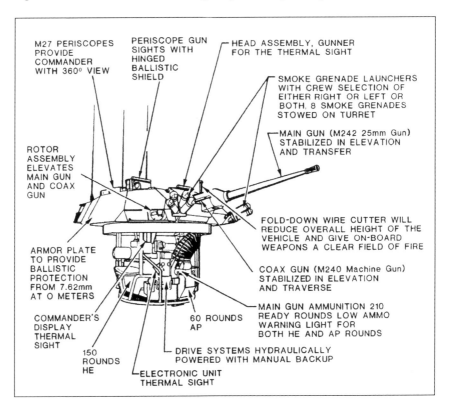

A detailed view of the LAV-25 turret. (DoD)

transmission (with five forward and one reverse gear) and 16 drive shafts to transfer engine power to the eight wheels and, for amphibious power, the two propellers. The vehicle can operate in four-wheel or eight-wheel drive. Tires are Michelin XL 11x16in tubeless steel belted radials, and the suspension consists of four front wheels using independent springs and shock absorbers, while the back four use torsion bars and shock absorbers. The driver has a steering wheel to control the front four tires.

The LAV-25 is an amphibious vehicle, capable of swimming in non-surf bodies of water. A steering arm connected to a rudder control cable operates the two propellers in conjunction with the steering wheel. This arm steers the vehicle on water in the same manner as on land. During amphibious operations, the LAV-25 uses a trim vane located at the front of the vehicle for stability; the trim vane, like the two propellers, can be engaged and disengaged from the driver's compartment.

In terms of performance, the LAV-25 has a maximum land speed of 62.2mph and a max water speed of 6.5mph. It has a 14.9in ground clearance and can climb at a maximum grade of 60 degrees and side slope of 30 degrees. The LAV-25's fully stabilized turret is armed with a 25mm M242 Bushmaster chain gun, a 7.62mm coaxial gun, and two M257 smoke grenade launchers on both sides of the turret. An additional pintle-mounted 7.62mm machine gun is located near the vehicle commander hatch.

The LAV-25 crew consists of a driver, gunner, and vehicle commander. The driver's position is located at the left front of the vehicle, adjacent to the

Marine LAV-25 crews from the 2nd LAV Battalion wait to load their vehicles onto an Air Force C-5 Galaxy at Robins Air Force Base, GA, for a flight to Marine Corps Air Station, Cherry Point, NC, March 1985. (DoD)

A Marine LAV-25 crew disembarks from a US Navy Landing Craft, Air Cushion (LCAC) in Maubara, Timor-Leste, while participating in Exercise *Marex*, October 14, 2009. The joint exercise promotes cooperation and training opportunities with the Australian and Timor-Leste military. To the right of the driver is a grill cover used to protect the LAV's engine during amphibious operations. The vehicle also wears a large protective cover over the M242 Bushmaster, M240 coaxial machine gun, and smoke grenade launchers. (DoD)

B LAV-25A2, QUANTICO (2011)

A Marine LAV-25A2 from Company D, 4th LAR Battalion, located at Camp Upshur, Marine Corps Base Quantico, Virginia, January 2011. This LAV-25A2 from the "Light Horse Marines" of 4th LAR is painted in the standard NATO scheme. The LAV-25A2 incorporates upgrades brought about by lessons learned in combat in Iraq and Afghanistan. External changes include an armor system designed to increase survivability against IEDs and kinetic energy weapons, and an upgraded suspension to handle the additional weight of the armor. Internal changes include an automatic fire suppression system and better ballistic protection within the hull. The turret has been upgraded and utilizes electric power to traverse, replacing the older hydraulic system. A Raytheon AN/PAS -13 ITSS allows for increased lethality in all-weather day/night conditions.

Key

1. Main gun (M242 25mm Automatic Cannon)
2. Gunner's station
3. Wire cutters
4. Gunner's periscope (1)
5. Pintle-mounted machine gun (M240E1, 7.62mm)
6. Fire suppression system (troop compartment)
7. Commander's station
8. Turret hatches
9. Commander's M27 periscopes (7)
10. Tool box & saw (troop compartment)
11. Troop compartment hatches
12. Bustle rack
13. Fuel filler cap
14. Troop seats
15. Rear doors
16. Rear door vision block
17. Twin rudders
18. Propeller
19. Spare tire
20. Emergency hatch
21. Driver's compartment
22. Towing lug
23. Tie-down lug
24. Trim vane
25. Left headlight cluster (contains headlight, blackout headlight, composite turn, park, and marker light)
26. Self recovery winch fairing
27. Tow rope
28. Self recovery winch & hatch
29. Driver's wire cutters
30. Driver's periscopes (3)
31. Engine compartment (6V53T Detroit Diesel)
32. Air inlet grill
33. Exhaust pipe & muffler
34. Driver's hatch
35. Air exhaust grill
36. Grenade launcher, for L8A1 smoke grenades

Specifications

Crew: 3 (commander, gunner, driver)
Combat weight: 28,100lb
Length overall: 252.6in
Width, overall: 98.4in
Height over turret: 100.9in
Maximum speed land: 62.2mph
Maximum speed water: 6.5mph
Maximum grade: 60 percent
Maximum side slope: 30 percent

vehicle's engine, while the commander and gunner positions are situated within the turret. The driver has a 180-degree view provided by three M17 periscopes. At night the driver can install a night vision periscope. The gunner sits on the left-side of the turret, with the vehicle commander's position on the right. The gunner has at his disposal a single M27 periscope to his left and a thermal sight in front of his position, while the vehicle commander has a periscope gun sight and seven M27 periscopes incorporated into the hatch. This arrangement provides a 360-degree view. In addition, the commander has a video display showing the view from the gunner's thermal sights.

The LAV-25 was designed to carry six troops within the rear hull; the Marine Corps typically seats four Marines scouts within this area. These scouts have two vision blocks on each side of the hull and troop compartment hatches overhead. When the troop compartment hatches are in the open position, sensors restrict the turret from firing over them, to protect those inside from muzzle blast. The LAV-25 was designed with two doors at the aft of the vehicle.

Armament

The main gun used by the LAV-25 is the M242 Automatic Cannon (Bushmaster) 25mm chain gun. Its design originated with the McDonnell Douglas Corporation, later Alliant Techsystems (ATK), and it utilizes a three-piece assembly (barrel, feeder, and receiver) that allows a single person to install or remove the main gun. A 1hp direct-current motor incorporated into the receiver drives a chain that actuates the gun's bolt; the gun operates mechanically, eliminating the need for a gas system to fire the weapon. Although the gun is fired utilizing electric power, it can also be fired manually if need be.

The M242 fires the NATO standard 25x137mm ammunition. Its dual-feed system allows the gunner to switch between armor-piercing and high-explosive rounds, and between three rates of fire: single shot; 100rpm at low rate; and 200rpm at high rate. The gun can be elevated to 60 degrees and depressed to minus 8 degrees. Maximum range is just over 11,000yds, with an effective range of 1,641yds. The LAV-25 turret at the ready carries 150 rounds of high-explosive and 60 rounds of armor-piercing ammunition, and an additional 420 rounds can be stowed in the hull.

Secondary armament consists of a 7.62mm M240 coaxial machine gun with 400 linked rounds and the option to carry a supplementary 7.62mm

Flying a red warning flag, an LAV-25 commander watches as his gunner fires the vehicle's 25mm Bushmaster chain gun on a live-fire range at Camp Pendleton, CA, 1984. The vehicle wears a distinctive four pattern camouflage scheme. (DoD)

An LAV-L accompanied by multiple light armored vehicles adorned with US flags roll into Kuwait International Airport, February 28, 1991. Painted on the front of the vehicle is a plus symbol followed by the letter "C," indicating a Navy corpsman is aboard. The length of rope draped across the front is utilized to assist stuck vehicles. (DoD)

pintle-mounted machine gun. The vehicle's ancillary equipment includes two M257 smoke grenade launchers located on each side of the turret. Each M257 carries four L8A1 smoke grenades, with a range of 45yds.

Marine Corps Variants
LAV-L (Logistics)

This logistics variant of the LAV was first produced in 1986. The LAV-L was designed with a raised roof to increase available storage space within the vehicle's hull, and it incorporates a two-section roof hatch that folds outward and a 1-ton chain hoist with a folding platform for the operator. Aft cargo doors use offset and overlapping hatches instead of the LAV-25's two separate hatches, allowing for unobstructed access for large pallets and oversized cargo.

The LAV-L operates with a three-man crew consisting of a driver and a commander, who are stationed in tandem on the left side of the vehicle, and a loadmaster who has a fold-down seat within the hull. Maximum payload is 2 tons, plus 1,440lb of ammunition. Armament consists of a pintle-mounted 7.62mm machine gun on the commander's cupola and like the combat variant it has two M257 smoke grenade launchers located on the raised roof on both sides of the vehicle.

A total of 94 LAV-L variants were produced during Fiscal Year 1985–86. Early versions of the LAV-L can be distinguished from late production models due to their sloped roofs. Marines from the 2nd Light Armored Infantry Battalion (2nd LAI) stationed out of Camp Lejeune were the first to use the LAV-L in combat alongside their LAV-25s during Operation *Just Cause*, the US invasion of Panama, in 1989.

LAV-R (Recovery)

Production of the LAV-R (Recovery) started in May 1986, and a total of 46 were built by the end of 1987. The LAV-R incorporates a roof-mounted hydraulic crane capable of lifting a maximum weight of 6,600lb; the crane can rotate 360 degrees. Outriggers and stabilizers are utilized when the crane is in use. Similar to the LAV-L, the recovery variant uses offset and overlapping hatches for unobstructed access. Its hull, however, was designed with interior lighting and a workbench for maintenance to be performed within the vehicle.

An LAV-R commander peers through binoculars for signs of enemy movement. The vehicle is littered with the basic essentials (water, fuel, and personal gear) in order for the crew to live out of the LAV for an extended period of time. (DoD)

A 30,000lb winch is mounted at the rear of the vehicle, and spades for the winch are stowed above the rear hatches.

The LAV-R is operated by a three-man crew consisting of a driver, commander, and rigger, with additional seating for two troops. Armament is similar to the LAV-L – a pintle-mounted 7.62mm machine gun on the commander's cupola and two M257 smoke grenade launchers located on the raised roof on both sides of the vehicle. Like the LAV-L, the LAV-R was deployed to Panama. Marines from the 2nd LAI utilized the LAV-R's ability to recover vehicles to dismantle Panamanian Defense Forces (PDF) roadblocks during Operation *Rough Rider*, clearing the way for the company's LAV-25s.

LAV-C2 (Command & Control)

The LAV-C2 command-and-control variant, with its vast array of communications equipment, affords the company commander a mobile command post. Similar to the LAV-L, the LAV-C2 has a raised roof for additional head room for the staff. The driver's position is standard to the LAV design, with the vehicle commander's seat situated just aft of the driver. The battalion commander's hatch (usually occupied by the battalion XO) is located on the left-hand side of the raised roof, directly behind the vehicle commander's position. At the right front of the hull is a seat for a staff officer; directly behind the staff seat are three radio operator positions. The radio operators have two hatches overhead and a map board on the right hull wall. The rear doors on the LAV-C2 utilize overlapping hatches similar to the LAV-L. Initial authorization to procure the C2 variant was completed during the 1985 Fiscal Year. By May of 1987, all 50 LAV-C2s had been completed. The C2 variant would first see combat action in 1989 during Operation *Just Cause* in Panama.

LAV-AT (Antitank)

The antitank variant of the LAV was first produced in 1987, with a total of 96 vehicles built. The vehicle incorporates the Emerson TOW (Tube-launched, Optically Tracked, Wire command-link guided missile) turret as its main armament. A total of 16 TOW missiles can be carried, 14 stowed in the vehicle's hull and two within the turret. The turret uses a AN/VVS-2(V)4 night sight, a 3x magnification wide-field-of-view telescope, and a 13x day sight tracker. In addition to the turret's optics, the gunner has seven vision blocks within the turret for a 280-degree field of view. An LAV-AT traditionally has a crew of four: a driver, commander, gunner, and loader. The loader could load the turret with TOW missiles under partial protection from the loader's hatch. Secondary armament for the vehicle consisted of a pintle-mounted 7.62mm machine gun on the commander's cupola and two M257 smoke grenade launchers located forward of the turret.

Marines make their way through a group of demonstrators during Operation *Uphold Democracy* in Haiti, 1994. Similar in appearance to the LAV-L, the C2 variant's three hatches/vision blocks and four antenna mounts located on each corner of the raised roof are key recognition features. (DoD)

LAV-M (Mortar)

The mortar variant of the LAV was intended for use with both the 81mm and the 107mm mortars, mounted on a turntable system mounted within the vehicle's hull. In order to fire the weapon from the vehicle, a three-section hatch was incorporated into the roof. The M252 (81mm) is the standard armament for the LAV-M, although 120mm mortars have been successfully test fired from the vehicle. The LAV-M crew consists of a driver, vehicle commander, and a three-man mortar team. The driver's compartment is similar to other variants. The vehicle commander is situated in a raised cupola located behind the driver, and he has a 7.62mm pintle-mounted machine gun for secondary armament and two M257 smoke grenade launchers. His station has eight M17 periscopes providing a 360-degree view. Ammunition for the 81mm is located on the left side of the vehicle, with space for 90 rounds. Folding troop seats on the right side of the vehicle are for the mortar team. In total, 50 LAV-M vehicles were eventually produced, with the last one rolling off the assembly line in late 1986.

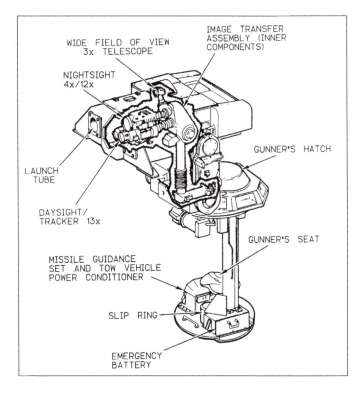

A closer look at the Emerson turret utilized on the LAV-AT reveals the reason why LAV crews relied on this variant for early warning of enemy movement. (DoD)

LAV-AD (Air Defense)

Both General Electric and the FMC Corporation were awarded contracts to build prototypes of an air defense variant of the LAV in December 1987. Each prototype was required to carry a 25mm main gun, a Stinger missile launcher, and 70mm Hydra rocket pod carrying seven unguided rockets. The FMC prototype utilized the M242 25mm chain gun with a higher rate of fire

A Marine LAV-AT crew moves into position to conduct weapons sighting operations in the Helmand Province of Afghanistan during Operation *Enduring Freedom*, June 19, 2008. The Marines were assigned to the 24th Marine Expeditionary Unit. (DoD)

Marines from Fox Company, 1st LAR Battalion, practice firing mortar rounds on a range at Al Asad Air Base, Iraq. The LAV-M crew serving as part of a weapons platoon was a reserve unit based out of Camp Lejeune, NC. (DoD)

than the standard LAV-25 weapon, along with four Stinger missiles and, for a time, seven 70mm Hydra unguided rockets. The General Electric Blazer turret used a GAU-12 25mm Equalizer five-barreled rotary cannon with a maximum rate of fire of 4,200rpm, the same weapon utilized by the AV-8B Harrier II and the US Air Force AC-130U gunship. Additional requirements included a Stinger launcher on the right and 70mm Hydra rockets on the left, astride the GAU-12. Five years after the initial awards were released, the DoD selected the General Electric (now General Dynamics) prototype. An additional Stinger launcher replaced the Hydra rocket pod after tests proved the unguided rockets were ineffective. The Marine Corps' initial plan to field 125 LAV-AD variants was drastically reduced to just 17, with the last vehicle delivered to the Marine Corps in 1998.

LAV-AG (Assault Gun)

As with the LAV-AD, an LAV-AG assault gun variant was planned with the original Marine Corps requirement. During the mid 1980s multiple weapon systems, including the Cockerill 90mm, M68 105mm, and the Ares XM274 75mm, were evaluated at the Army's Proving Ground in Aberdeen, Maryland, to no avail. It was not until General Motors installed and tested the Benét Laboratories EX35 105mm low-recoil gun that a contract was awarded. Cadillac Gage Textron received the award in 1990 to produce

A Marine from the 1st LAR Battalion prepares an 81mm mortar round inside an LAV-M during field operations on Camp Pendleton, CA, April 21, 2005. (DoD)

three prototypes utilizing the EX35, which reduced the recoil effects that plagued earlier attempts but did not reduce the firepower performance. Designated the LAV-105, the vehicle featured a new turret design to house an automatic loader. Funding issues later cancelled the project in 1991, only for it to be resurrected again in 1993. Test results obtained while firing the main gun on the move and in a stationary position passed all the Marine Corps requirements. Ultimately, due to funding issues no production contract was awarded.

The prototype General Electric air defense turret is adorned with confirmed kills of both aerial drones and ground targets. An initial production run of 125 LAV-ADs was cut to only 17. The Marine Corps LAV-AD variant was the last of the first-generation LAVs to be produced for the Marine Corps. (DoD)

MEWSS (Mobile Electronic Warfare System)

A unique LAV variant within the Marine Corps inventory is the MEWSS, specializing in jamming enemy communications (VHF and FM transmissions). The Marine Corps tested two prototypes in 1986. After these tests successfully met the requirement for an electronic warfare (EW) platform, the Corps purchased a dozen vehicles, with the last being delivered in 1989. The vehicles were destined for the two Marine Corps radio battalions, with each battalion receiving a total of six vehicles. The EW variant has an interesting crew make-up: all crew positions are filled by EW operators instead of traditional 0313 LAV crews.

The MEWSS is similar to the LAV-C2 in that it has a raised roof and utilizes hatches for the rear crew positions. The driver's position is standard, with the vehicle commander's position just aft of the driver. The commander has five M17 periscopes incorporated into his cupola. Two EW operator positions are located on the right side of the hull facing the EW suite situated on the vehicle's left bulkhead. Three vision blocks are located in the crew compartment, and a third seat is situated facing the rear of the vehicle at the front of the compartment.

In order to fulfill its mission of EW attacks and data collection, the MEWSS has a vast array of EW equipment: a signal jammer (AN/ULQ-19) and two acquisition receivers (W-J 8618B), and a directional finder

An LAV-AD crew from the 4th LAR Battalion fire their 25mm Gatling gun during a live-fire exercise at Fort Hunter, CA, during Exercise *Highland Thunder*, March 10, 1999. The General Electric Blazer turret utilized the GAU-12 25mm Gatling gun and two quadruple FIM-92 Stinger launchers. (DoD)

(AN/PRD-10) that consists of a large antenna and mast positioned on the roof of the vehicle. The vehicle utilizes two air conditioning systems, one powered by the vehicle's engine, a second electrically powered. Armament consists of a 7.62mm pintle-mounted machine gun and two M257 smoke grenade launchers.

Variant Type	Numbers produced (1984–2003)
LAV-25	467
LAV-C2	55
LAV-L	109
LAV-R	45
LAV-AT	115
LAV-M	60
LAV-MEWSS	12
LAV-AD	17
Total	880

Source: *Jane's Armor and Artillery 2005–06*

Upgrades

An up-armored program was successfully completed in April 1991 utilizing Light Appliqué System Technique (LAST) ceramic tile armor kits developed by the Foster–Miller Inc. The $2 million contract was awarded for 75 prototype kits to add additional armor for LAVs deploying to Saudi Arabia. The appliqué armor within the LAST kits utilizes a hook and loop attachment system and can be installed by the crew to add protection from .50-caliber/12.7mm and 14.5mm rounds. Yet the kits were developed too late to see action during Operation *Desert Storm* in 1991. After the war, the LAST kits were split, equipping Marine LAV units on the East and West Coasts.

In 1998, Marine LAV units started to receive passive armor systems with protection against 20mm armor-piercing rounds fired from 15m away. Known as the Composite Ceramic Armor (CCA) system, the kits were produced by the Ordnance Systems Division of Rafael, Israel.

A Marine MEWSS crew assigned to Task Force Tarawa takes up a defensive position within a 360-vehicle formation – the formation allows for 360 degrees of observation. The Marines were participating in Operation *Southern Scimitar*, with the intention of removing insurgents from the area. (DoD)

A Marine scout from the 3rd LAR Battalion is followed by his LAV-25A2 while searching for weapon caches outside Combat Outpost Rawah, Iraq, February 1, 2008. (DoD)

SLEP

In 2000, the Marine Corps selected Metric Systems of Fort Walton Beach, Florida, to perform a Service Life Extension Program (SLEP) for the branch's remaining 770 LAVs. The program was initiated to increase survivability, reliability, and bring down the operational and support costs. To increase the LAV survivability, add-on camouflage panels were used to reduce the vehicle's visual signature, as well as heat emissions. The vehicle's exhaust system was treated to improve thermal reduction. Electrical and electronic systems with high failure rates were upgraded, and corrosion control was improved, decreasing the operational cost per vehicle. A heads-up display (HUD) was integrated into the driver's compartment to improve safety during operations. LAVs assigned to fleet locations had the SLEP kits installed by contractors. Depot personnel located at Albany, Georgia, and Barstow, California, would also install the SLEP kits as needed when an LAV underwent inspections. Once an LAV had received the SLEP upgrades, it was designated an LAV-A1, the first of which was ready for service in May 2003.

LAV-A2 Program

In 2005 a Marine Corps force structure review board added five companies to the four LAR battalions, with a goal of increasing the LAV inventory to 1,005 vehicles. Additional procurement began in 2006, with 125 vehicles needed to field the additional companies. The new vehicles would incorporate lessons learned from experiences in Iraq and Afghanistan, these conflicts contributing to significant survivability upgrades within the Marine Corps' LAV program. The changes gave the vehicle a new A2 designation. The A2's external changes include a three-kit armor system designed to increase survivability against improvised explosive devices (IEDs) and kinetic energy weapons. The additional weight of the new armor dictated a change in the LAV's suspension. The upgraded suspension consists of improved shocks, struts, torsion bars, drive shafts, and steering knuckles. Internal changes include an automatic fire suppression system and better ballistic protection within the hull. The turret upgrade utilizes electric power to traverse, replacing the hydraulic system. A Raytheon AN/PAS-13 Improved Thermal Sight System (ITSS) allows for increased lethality in all-weather day/night conditions. The sight incorporates a new laser rangefinder, fire-control solutions, and improved target acquisition, giving the A2 enhanced first-hit

Marines from 1st LAR Battalion prepare to move out in their LAV-25A2 to the range on Al Asad Air Base. The Marines first have to calibrate the sights on their small-arms prior to going on real-world operations, February 2, 2009. (DoD)

performance. In February 2006, a contract was awarded to General Dynamics to produce the LAV-A2s, with multiple variants, the first of which was accepted on October 12, 2007. The majority of the 893 LAV vehicles within the Marine Corps' inventory as of 2011 have been brought up from the LAV-A1 baseline to the A2 standard. The last of the LAV-A1 variants within the inventory will be upgraded as they are rotated from maritime prepositioning ships.

ASLAV-25 (Australian Light Armored Vehicle-25)

The Australian LAV can trace its beginnings to the success of the Marine Corps LAV-25 program. In 1990 the Australian government procured 15 vehicles from the US Marine Corps (14 LAV-25s and a single LAV-R). The vehicles were evaluated by Alpha Squadron, 2nd Cavalry Regiment, in order to develop maintenance and operating procedures as well as defining vehicle modifications needed for Australian use. The second phase of the ASLAV program began in 1992, when the Australian Defence Material Organisation (DMO) signed an agreement to purchase 113 vehicles and support equipment. By 1997, all 113 vehicles were completed. Phase 3 of the ASLAV program bought another

AUSTRALIAN AND US LAVS, 2008 AND 2010

1: An Australian Army ASLAV from the 2nd Mentoring and Reconstruction Task Force during Operation *Slipper*, January 21, 2010. Operating in Afghanistan's Oruzgan Province presented some of the harshest conditions for the soldiers and their ASLAV, with relentless dust and bitter cold nights. The crew of this ASLAV have placed a small cover on the muzzle of the M242 Bushmaster chain gun to keep the weapon clean. The red kangaroo painted on the hull is nearly impossible to make out on this vehicle due to the caked-on dirt. A bright orange fabric panel can be seen directly behind the turret; this piece of equipment is a signal maker, utilized to alert coalition aircraft that the vehicle is friendly.

2: A Marine LAV from Company D, 1st Light Armored Reconnaissance Battalion, Iraq. On November 10, 2008, the "Diablos" relieved soldiers from the 3rd Armored Cavalry Regiment, who had previously operated within the Nineweh Province of Iraq. The Marines from Company D were utilized to kick off Operation *Defeat Al Qaeda in the North II*, aimed at destroying foreign fighters and local insurgency operations west of the city of Mosul. The Marine LAVs are just one part of the combined arms team that makes up the MAGTF. The company's new LAV-A2s are a vast improvement over the original LAV-25. Due to lessons learned from earlier operations in Iraq, the new vehicles incorporate additional armored plating for the hull and turret for improved protection from IEDs, as well as updated optics and suspension.

1

2

An Australian ASLAV crosses one of the numerous rivers running through the Oruzgan Province, southern Afghanistan. The crew is conducting a patrol with Dutch troops near the village of Chora. Unlike the Canadian Coyote, the Australian ASLAV retained the ability to conduct amphibious operations. (ADF)

144 vehicles for the Australian Army, plus required that all Phase 2 vehicles be brought up to Phase 3 standard. The Phase 3 upgrades included an integrated laser rangefinder, electric turret drives, improved thermal sights, and upgraded suspension. Australian Army ASLAV-25s and support variants have seen combat action both in Iraq and Afghanistan since 2001.

LAV-25 Reconnaissance (Coyote)

The Canadian government's need to replace its inventory of aging Lynx tracked reconnaissance vehicles led to the procurement of the Coyote Reconnaissance vehicle (based on the LAV-25 design). Canadian armed forces eventually purchased 203 vehicles with two separate surveillance kits envisioned (Battle Group Kit and Fixed Brigade Kit).

The LAV-25 Coyote differs from its Marine Corps cousin in many ways. First and foremost, the Coyote is not amphibious; the vehicle was procured without a trim vane and twin propellers. Second, the troop compartment at the rear of the hull in Marine Corps LAV-25s is utilized as a surveillance compartment by the Canadian Coyote. Instead of 4–6 troops, the compartment is occupied by a single surveillance operator.

Two Royal Canadian Dragoon Coyotes conduct reconnaissance for the 1st Battalion, Royal Canadian Regiment, on the Kosovo/Serbian border during a NATO peacekeeping mission, May 16, 2000. The vehicle's surveillance system can detect, monitor, and record enemy activity up to 15 miles away, day or night, and in adverse weather. (CAF)

The LAV-25 utilizing the Fixed Brigade Kit uses a sensor module mounted on an electrically operated telescopic mast, elevated from the left troop compartment with the hatch in the open position. The mast can elevate the sensor suite 33ft above the vehicle. The surveillance equipment consists of a thermal imager, battlefield surveillance radar, day or night long-range camera, and laser rangefinder. The second variation (the Battle Group Kit) utilizes surveillance sensors mounted on a tripod. The system is manportable and can be deployed 218yds from the vehicle. The sensor suite consists of a laser rangefinder, long-range TV camera, and a thermal imager. Canada has deployed LAV-25 Coyotes for operations in the Balkans, multiple countries in Africa, Haiti, and Afghanistan. Thirteen Coyotes were fitted with the Ferret Small Arms Detectors before deploying to Afghanistan. This system allows the crew to detect small-arms fire, providing information on the caliber, bearing, and range of the incoming rounds.

The Coyote's troop compartment houses a single surveillance operator in place of scout troops. The operator controls a mast-mounted surveillance system to provide security for Forward Operating Base (FOB) Robinson west of Kandahar. 1 May 2006. (CAF)

Saudi Arabian National Guard (SANG) LAV-25

In 1990, Saudi Arabia looked to procure LAVs through the US Foreign Military Sales (FMS) program. The LAVs would replace SANG's aging V-150 Commando four-wheeled armored fighting vehicles (AFVs). The Saudi government eventually placed an order for 1,117 LAVs. One of the most interesting variants procured for SANG was the LAV-AG (Assault Gun). The variant similar to the Marine Corps requirement (which failed to reach production due to funding issues) was finally ordered in 1999 by Saudi Arabia. One-hundred and thirty LAV-AGs would eventually be produced by General Motors of Canada (now General Dynamics Land Systems-Canada). The SANG assault gun variant was armed with a 90mm Cockerill Mk 8 Gun system, utilizing a two-man turret. A wide variety of ammunition is produced in Belgium for the Mk 8 weapon system, ammunition types consist of High-Explosive Plastic (HEP), Armor-Piercing Fin-Stabilized Discarding-Sabot Tracer (APFSDS-T), Target-Practice Tracer (TP-T), and Smoke.

OPERATIONS

Panama

Although the LAV-25 was initially developed in response to tensions in the Middle East, the weapon system would first see combat action in Central America. Marines from the 2nd LAI Battalion were sent to Panama from May 1989 to June 1990. The LAV companies deployed were reinforcements operating under control of Marine Forces Panama (MARFORP). Their non-combat role in the early stages was to allow freedom of movement for Americans living in Panama. This meant constant interaction with Dictator Manuel Noriega's PDF. When H-Hour came with the beginning of Operation *Just Cause* on December 20, 1989, the conflict became hot and combat operations to hunt down Noriega commenced.

An LAV-25 commander goes over a map with the vehicle's gunner while conducting maneuvers in Panama. Early on, LAV-25s utilized M60E3 machine guns for the pintle mount. The M60E3 was later replaced with the M240, already in use for the LAV's coaxial armament. (DoD)

Company A (Reinforced), from the 2nd LAI, was the first to deploy LAVs to Panama, on May 12, 1989. Alpha Company operated 14 LAV-25s, two LAV-Ls and a single LAV-C2 variant. Ten four-man scout teams were assigned to the unit: three teams per platoon, plus one assigned to the headquarters section. The Marines from Company A participated in Operation *Nimrod Dancer* Phase I. This mission provided security for US citizens, and property, and enforced the 1977 Panama Canal Treaty. Initial missions consisted of reconnaissance, US Army convoy escorts, and mounted and dismounted security.

During Operation *Big Show*, Marines from 2nd LAI swam their LAVs to the eastern shore of the Panama Canal, making it difficult for the PDF to observe and follow the Marines' movements. The mission was followed by a night swim of the canal under complete radio silence and blacked-out conditions. Then on August 8, Operation *Westward Ho* began. LAVs from the 2nd LAI conducted a route reconnaissance mission from Empire Range to Rodman Naval Station. During this mission, PDF forces detained a Marine LAV-L in Arraijan. Marines sent a reinforcing platoon to free the blocked vehicle. In the ensuing confrontation, the Americans extricated the LAV-L and captured 29 personnel, including Major Sierro (Manuel Noriega's brother-in-law) as well as the Mayor of Arraijan.

Operation *Nimrod Dancer* Phase II started on August 7, 1989. Tactical control of LAI operations fell to Company B, 2nd LAI, on August 11; the company utilized the 17 vehicles left over from the previous unit. In respect of local laws enacted to protect roads from damage, American officials prohibited tracked vehicles like the Army's M113 from conducting missions through towns. The Marine Corps' LAV had no restrictions owing to its wheeled design.

The LAV-25 first saw combat action during Operation *Just Cause*, December 1989. The Panamanians labeled the LAVs "Tanquitos," meaning little tanks. An LAV-25 from Delta Company, 2nd LAI, makes a profound impression on the Panamanian Defense Forces while guarding a street in Panama City, December 1989. (DoD)

On October 26, Company D departed for Panama to replace Company B. The Marines from Company D brought with them the first replacement LAVs. The unit operated 14 LAV-25s, two LAV-Ls, and one LAV-R. Key personnel from the unit accompanied Company B on routine vehicle patrols during their last missions. The company conducted a small exercise on

November 22, Operation *Rough Rider*, to familiarize the LAV crews with the area of operation. The route passed through four major towns. On their way back to Rodman Naval Station, the Marines faced a PDF roadblock on Thatcher Highway. The PDF were given five minutes to clear the roadblock. After the five minutes passed, the commander of Company D, Captain Gerald H. Gaskins, ordered his LAV drivers to button up and gunners to ready their machine guns. As the company passed through the roadblock, a Panamanian pickup truck rammed an LAV-L, puncturing the right front tire. The LAV-L continued on past the roadblock and was repaired in a matter of minutes.

Operation *Just Cause*

H-Hour for Operation *Just Cause* was set for 0100hrs on December 20, 1989. MARFORP ordered Company D to assault and secure a radio station in Arraijan (DNTT Number 2 station). The LAV-25 crews were restricted from using their 25mm Bushmasters on the station in the belief that the station's communication equipment could be used to monitor PDF traffic. The lead vehicle drove through a locked fence at the station and started to receive small-arms fire. Its coaxial and pintle-mounted machine guns provided cover for the scout teams. A Fleet Anti-terrorist Security Team (FAST) team attached to Company D, trained to fight in urban environments, helped secure the station. Scout team member Corporal Garreth Isaak lost his life during the firefight; he would earn the Silver Star (posthumous) for his actions. The company turned to Peredes Headquarters. The FAST teams, using stun grenades, forced the five Panamanians occupying the station to surrender.

The 1st and 3rd Platoons cut all access into the city of Arraijan. After the teams were in position, a previously slow-moving civilian vehicle accelerated towards the LAVs. The FAST teams opened up on the vehicle, killing the driver. A second vehicle attempted to escape the Marine perimeter, with little success.

The Marines were also given the mission to secure the 10th Military Zone Headquarters in La Chorrera by MARFORP. An estimated 150–200 enemy troops garrisoned the headquarters, which consisted of four buildings surrounded by a 6ft concrete wall with firing ports. The forces tasked to secure the buildings included 31 dismounted Marines. With no fire support

An LAV-25 from Alpha Company, 2nd LAI Battalion, patrols a road along the Panama Canal. Alpha Company's main mission was to ensure freedom of movement for American forces in and around the Canal Zone, May 1989. (DoD)

available, the Marine LAV crews became the supporting arm of the attack. En route to the headquarters, an OH-58 crew reported a PDF roadblock composed of civilian buses. Two LAV-25s approached the roadblock side by side at top speed while firing their 25mm main guns – the Panamanians quickly abandoned their position. A Virginia Air National Guard A-7 Corsair II then arrived to provide air support. After the A-7 strike, the Marines assaulted the headquarters, and heavy fire from their LAV-25s soon pummeled the buildings into unrecognizable piles of rubble.

In the weeks that followed, Marines from Company D and the FAST teams cleared nearly 50 buildings. Reflecting on the LAV's role in Panama operations, Captain Gerald H. Gaskins remarked that "It was important to be able to provide support to the dismounted infantry to reduce the amount of exposure to enemy fire during the assault. The speed and agility of the wheeled LAV made it a champion in Panama City with high speed and mobility over the assortment of improved and unimproved roads."

Operation *Desert Shield/Storm*

On August 2, 1990, Iraq's Ba'athist dictator, Saddam Hussein, ordered his forces to invade and occupy the country of Kuwait. President George Bush ordered US forces into the theater to protect Kuwait's neighbors to the south. Most vulnerable were the Kingdom of Saudi Arabia, Bahrain, Qatar, Oman, and the United Arab Emirates (UAE). The threat from the east was so

D LAV-25S IN PANAMA (1989) AND OPERATION *DESERT STORM* (1991)

1: A Marine LAV-25 from Company A (Reinforced), 2nd LAI Battalion, is here seen during freedom-of-movement operations near the Canal Zone, Panama, months prior to Operation *Just Cause*. The Panamanians labeled the Marine LAVs "Tanquitos," meaning "little tanks." The vehicles' versatility made it difficult for PDF to shadow the vehicles. On May 28, LAV-25s crews participated in Operation *Big Show* and used the opportunity to swim the Panama Canal from west to east, ending their amphibious maneuver on the shores of Panama City, thus catching the PDF off guard. Marines from Company A took part in the initial deployment of Marine LAVs into Panama. The company's equipment consisted of 14 LAV-25s, two LAV-L logistic variants, and one LAV-C2 command-and-control variant. This vehicle's exterior remains relatively clean of stowage, with some personal gear stowed behind the commander's and gunner's hatches. The commander's pintle mount is occupied by an M60 machine gun, readied with live 7.62mm ammunition. Directly in front of the driver's compartment a small panel remains partially open, concealing the vehicle's self-recovery winch inside. Rolled up to the left of the driver's hatch is the engine's grill cover, utilized during amphibious operations and adverse weather to protect the vehicle's engine.

2: A Marine LAV-25 seen during the final drive into Kuwait International Airport during Operation *Desert Storm*. Marine LAVs assigned to Task Force Shepherd entered Kuwait City during the final push towards Phase Line Green, the preplanned limit of the 1st Marine Division's advance. The crews faced little opposition as they reached their objective, as the majority of Iraqi Forces had retreated back into Iraq. The crew of this particular LAV-25 attached a small American flag to one of their antenna masts. It was not uncommon to see Marine LAVs flying the Stars and Stripes, Marine Corps Colors, or even state flags from their turrets during the final days of *Desert Storm*. Painted on the side of the turret and the hull of the vehicle is an inverted "V" to designate the vehicle as friendly. During the ground war, fratricide was one of the greatest dangers facing coalition ground forces. The Marines of Task Force Shepherd had already lost crews to friendly fire during the battle for OP-4 in January. In one incident, an LAV-AT accidently fired on another LAV-AT, killing the entire crew, and in a second incident a USAF A-10 Thunderbolt II accidently destroyed an LAV-25 during the same fight (the driver was the only survivor). It was after events like this that Central Command ordered the use of inverted "V" markings on all coalition vehicles. Vehicles were also adorned with bright orange signal panels to alert allied air crews that a vehicle was friendly. Marine Corps camouflage schemes during *Desert Storm* varied from the traditional NATO scheme to vehicles painted in a solid coat of tan. This particular vehicle had green portions of the standard NATO scheme painted over with tan to better adapt to the environment.

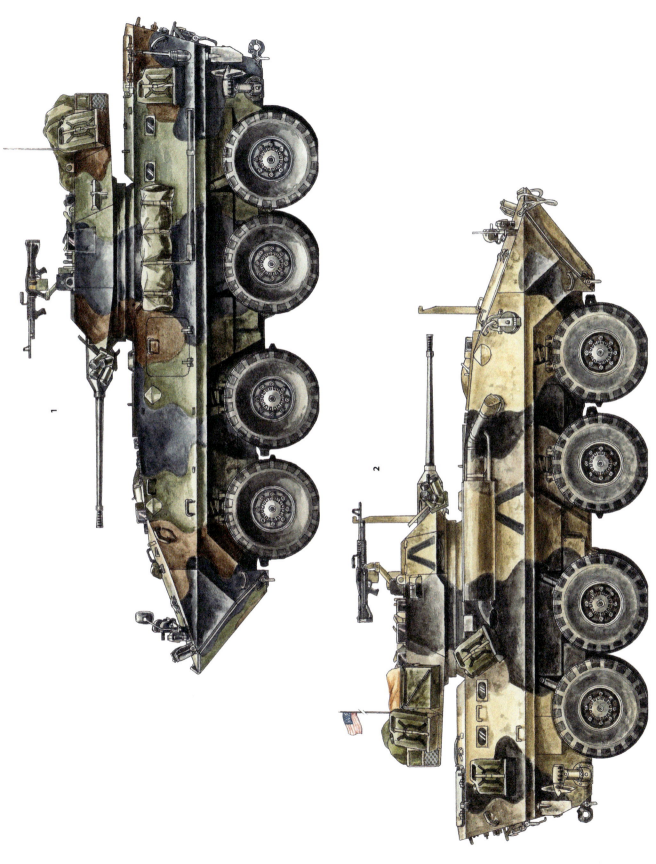

A Marine LAV-25 assigned to the 2nd Marine Division prepares to board a Maritime Prepositioning Ship (MPS) at Morehead City, NC, in preparation for Operation *Desert Shield*. (DoD).

imminent that for the first time in the country's 58-year existence, Saudi Arabia permitted foreign troops to be stationed on its soil.

After taking Kuwait by force, Iraqi forces looking to defend their newly acquired territory began constructing a defense network of barriers, minefields, and fortifications 1.5–9 miles inside Kuwait, paralleling the Saudi border. To secure their border, the Saudis had constructed their own series of earthen barriers 16ft high years before the Iraqi invasion took place. The Saudi barriers, known to the coalition forces within that sector as "The Berm," had police outposts every 19 miles. These observation posts (OPs) would become the backdrop on which Marine LAV crews would first take on Iraqi Forces.

Organizational structure

During Operation *Desert Storm*, elements of all four Marine LAI battalions would see combat. Marine units, including LAV companies from both the 1st, 2nd, and 3rd LAI Battalions, were organized within task forces. The 4th LAI units were attached to the 5th Marine Expeditionary Brigade (5th MEB). The task force organizational structure was established by Lieutenant Colonel Clifford O. Myers, Commanding Officer (CO), 1st LAI Battalion. Marine LAVs were to be utilized in the traditional cavalry role, and would provide the screening force for I Marine Expeditionary Force (I MEF) main body.

By the start of the ground war, I MEF had 301 LAVs in-theater. The US Army also operated a small number of LAV-25s on loan from the Marine Corps. The Army's 3rd Battalion, 73rd Armored Regiment, of the 82nd Airborne Division deployed 14 LAV-25s and one LAV-R in conjunction with their M551 Sheridan tanks during *Desert Storm*.

LAVS by type/quantity, assigned to I MEF	
LAV-25	150
LAV-AT	48
LAV-L	38
LAV-C2	25
LAV-M	18

OP-4 and the Iraqi Offensive

On January 29, 1991, Iraqi forces launched a multi-pronged attack to break through the OPs and take the towns of Kibrit, Khafji, and Mishab. Observation Post Four (OP-4) had a main building with two tower structures. At the time of the attack a platoon of Marines from the 1st Recon Battalion occupied the post. The platoon had a 5-ton truck and three HMWWVs situated in a horseshoe berm used as their rallying point. At the outpost, the recon Marines could call upon Company D's two platoons of LAVs, which had arrived near the OP that day. Company D's CO, Captain Roger L. Pollard, had 13 LAV-25s, seven LAV-ATs, and a LAV-C2 at his disposal.

An M551 Sheridan follows an Army LAV-25 during training near Khalid Range, Saudi Arabia, January 10, 1991. The US Army's 3rd Battalion, 73rd Armored Regiment, of the 82nd Airborne Division operated 14 LAV-25s and one LAV-R on loan from the Marine Corps during *Desert Storm*. (DoD)

Marine spotters utilizing night-vision scopes located 30 enemy vehicles moving towards their OP. The Marines estimated that the approaching force contained five T-62 tanks and multiple BMP infantry fighting vehicles (IFVs). Immediately the Recon platoon called for an airstrike. An airstrike failed to stop the Iraqi advance, and the enemy vehicles entered the range of small-arms fire from the observation post. The recon Marines stopped one of the approaching tanks with an LAW rocket.

Captain Pollard spotted the enemy formation at 1926hrs, and put his crews on full alert. He organized an attack formation consisting of 13 LAV-25s plus three LAV-ATs, and a second formation of four LAV-ATs for support. The company's XO manned the LAV-C2 in back of the frontline. Task Force Shepherd CO Lieutenant Colonel Clifford O. Myers instructed the company commander not to take action until the enemy made clear its intentions. As the firefight between the recon Marines and Iraqi armor started, their intentions could not have been clearer. Once the Iraqi armor came within range, the LAVs opened up and immediately knocked out an Iraqi tank. The stricken tank burned brightly, creating a reference point for other LAV crews. Three T-55 tanks engaged the recon Marines, who were now nearly out of anti-tank munitions.

A Marine from the 1st LAI Battalion prepares ammunition for the LAV-25's coaxial machine gun and the M242 Bushmaster during Operation *Desert Shield*, October 1990. (DoD)

Turret art was not uncommon during Operation *Desert Storm*. This LAV-25 named "CROAKER" was from Charlie Company, 2nd LAI Battalion. (DoD)

By 2130hrs, main gun fire from Iraqi tanks forced the Marines occupying the post to abandon their defense. Company D's commander attempted to rescue the recon Marines through a counterattack by 2nd Platoon. He halted the platoon and instructed the crews to fire TOW missiles at the advancing Iraqi armor. The explosion that erupted confirmed some initial success; one of their vehicles, however, an LAV-AT, had been hit as well in the exchange. "The explosion was so violent we couldn't tell which hog had been hit," Captain Pollard later explained. "I thought we had been hit by Saggers fired by the Iraqi tanks."

The XO in the LAV-C2, situated between the two platoons, reported that an LAV-AT of 1st Platoon had fired on the 2nd Platoon LAV-AT. The missile penetrated the rear hatch where TOW missiles were stowed within the hull, and the detonation killed the LAV-AT crew instantly. Marine fire destroyed a second T-55 soon after, which in turn stalled the Iraqi advance, giving Company D time to regroup. As Company D's fight continued, Pollard became reluctant to utilize any more TOW missiles and reconfigured his formation with the emphasis on the LAV-25s. He used the thermal and night sights on the LAV-ATs to help get his LAV-25s on target. When an LAV-25 found a target, all of the LAV-25s within range would join in. This tactic also outlined the enemy vehicle for air support within the area of OP-4. Although 25mm high-explosive rounds could not penetrate the armor of a T-55, repeated strikes against a tank's armor sometimes caused its Iraqi crewmembers to "bug out." When several Iraqi tanks attempted to flank their position, Company D adjusted and reluctantly fired a second volley of TOW missiles.

After the TOW shots, the company moved back and called in a section of A-10 Thunderbolt II aircraft. The battle had now lasted nearly two hours. One of the A-10 pilots could not visually locate the tracers bouncing off a T-55's turret. The lead A-10 pilot radioed that he intended to drop a flare for the forward air controller (FAC) to use as a reference to get the section back on target. The flare fell directly behind an LAV-25. The FAC gave the position of a T-55 to the northeast when a huge explosion ripped through the platoon. "I was in the center of the line looking for the flare to land in front of me, when all of a sudden there was this huge explosion on my right," Captain Pollard recalled. "I thought we had been flanked and had lost a vehicle to enemy tank fire." Instead, a second A-10 had accidentally destroyed the LAV-25 after the first A-10 deployed its flare.

Having lost contact with the enemy and with a second LAV destroyed, Company D needed to regroup. The first battle for OP-4 ended soon after the second friendly fire incident. In all the LAV crews and close air support stopped the Iraqi advance on OP-4, but at a high cost to the Marines.

Iraqi forces tested both OP-5 and OP-6 during the battle. Captain Thomas P. Protzeller's Company C was in the area. The situation turned hot at 0110hrs when Iraqi artillery targeted OP-6. After an initial artillery barrage lifted, an Iraqi mechanized assault began. A dozen vehicles dropped off Iraqi troops at OP-6, which the Americans had abandoned early on. Company C's commander observed a force of 50–75 vehicles in support of the assault troops. The Marines called in a series of air strikes against the vehicles while Company C moved closer to OP-6. Just after the company was in position, 20 Iraqi vehicles assaulted the formation. Marine TOW missiles destroyed 11 enemy vehicles.

Captain Shupp's Company A was ordered to take Company D's position at OP-4. They looked for survivors of the A-10 friendly fire incident and found the driver of Red Two (its call sign) alive but wounded. The crews noticed a large formation of Iraqi vehicles on the Kuwait side of the border. Instead of waiting for another attack on OP-4, Captain Shupp had his LAV-ATs fire a volley of TOW missiles, destroying two tanks. He then sent a platoon to look for the LAV-AT (call sign Green Two) missing from the first engagement. When the Marines finally found the burnt-out hulk of the LAV-AT they confirmed there were no survivors. The fight for OP-4 wore on as the Iraqis continued to send troops and vehicles into the area. Shupp worked with AH-1W Super Cobra helicopters, taking out three more Iraqi tanks. Iraqi infantry stormed into OP-4 just as two Iraqi tanks arrived. The momentary lack of air support and numerical superiority forced the Marines to break contact.

Air support arrived in the form of USAF A-10 Thunderbolt IIs and later F/A-18 Hornets, allowing Shupp the opportunity to get Company A back into the fight. He brought his formations close enough for the LAV-ATs to get into action. In broad daylight, 18 Iraqi T-55 tanks exchanged fire with Company A's LAV-25s and LAV-ATs. The LAV-25s could not penetrate the tanks' armor, but their maneuverability kept the Iraqi armor busy while the LAV-ATs and coalition aircraft targeted the enemy. Main gun fire from a T-55 or T-62 could have easily destroyed an LAV, with its thin armor, but the Iraqi crews were poorly trained and badly led. Although the Iraqis also had supporting fire from artillery, they failed to register any damage on the LAVs. To the Marines' surprise, the T-55s and T-62s withdrew further into Kuwait. Company B and Company D were brought up to

A HMWWV and an LAV-25 named "GUNSLINGER" stand perimeter watch after a recent weapons seizure from the forces of Somali warlord General Aideed. The Marine LAV-25 driver watches vigilantly through a pair of binoculars while the commander mans the M240 machine gun, January 1992. At the back of the turret, the vehicle displays a bright orange VS-17 signal marker to help identify itself as friendly to aircraft. (DoD)

the berm to reinforce Company C's position. In all 22 Iraqi tanks were destroyed during the battle.

The engagement at OP-4 uncovered multiple issues for coalition forces, and revealed that military intelligence strongly overestimated the enemy's capabilities before the battle. For the coalition, the lack of aerial surveillance allowed large armored formations to set up positions on the Kuwait border. The two friendly-fire incidents had an immediate impact on all allied forces. Central Command ordered the use of inverted "V" markings on all coalition vehicles. Vehicles were also adorned with bright orange signal panels to alert allied air crews that a vehicle was friendly.

Into Kuwait

In preparation for the upcoming offensive, LAVs from the 2nd LAI Battalion were inside the Kuwait border on G-minus 3. (G-Day is the day on which an order is given to deploy a unit.) They served as a diversionary force to draw away Iraqi forces from the actual breach site. As for Task Force Shepherd, all but one company of LAVs from the task force were attached to various other units. The LAVs provided screening for other task forces within the division preparing to breach the Iraqi defenses. Lieutenant Colonel Myers had Company B at his disposal for only a short time. Companies A and C would eventually return to Task Force Shepherd, as well as Company D, which was re-assigned to Task Force Ripper.

On G-Day (February 24), Task Force Shepherd cleared the first obstacle belt without resistance, and linked up with Company C's LAV that had been released from screening for Task Force Taro. As the LAVs from Task Force Shepherd reached the second obstacle belt, they encountered a bottleneck of vehicles waiting to get through their specific lanes. The LAV crews found fresh tracks passing through a minefield and used them to proceed past this second obstacle. The task force attacked Iraqi artillery positions while covering for Task Force Ripper, and the LAVs of Task Force Shepherd established a screen line that skirted the western edge of the Al Burqan oilfields. En route the crews were the first US ground forces to encounter the burning Iraqi oilfields, which created a surreal scene, with visibility at times less than 50yds and hordes of surrendering Iraqi troops coming forward.

Still wearing the desert camouflage scheme from Operation *Desert Storm*, a Marine LAV-25 crew provides security at Mogadishu Airport, Somalia, during Operation *Restore Hope*. An Air Force C-141B Starlifter can be seen in the background. (DoD)

Companies C and D, both recently returned to Task Force Shepherd, encountered Iraqi T-62s and destroyed a combined total of 11 tanks.

New intelligence gained by Task Force Ripper shed light on a possible Iraqi counterattack coming from the Al Burqan oilfields. After receiving further information, Myers established a screen, emphasizing antitank weapons with their advanced sights towards the front. General Myatt's division headquarters was near the frontline and requested reinforcements from one of the LAV units. Company B was selected and linked up with Company C of the 1st Battalion, 1st Marines, already in the vicinity. Members of Company B did not appreciate this assignment, since their company had seen little action during the OP-4 engagement and G-Day. Now for all intents and purposes, guarding the division HQ did not seem to promise enemy action. When Captain Eddie S. Ray, Company B's commander, requested his unit be sent back to the screen line, his appeal was denied. What he could not know was that Company B's position would become vital to the division's most important engagement of the war.

Not long after his company was in place, one of Captain Ray's LAV-25s accidentally discharged a round of 25mm ammunition into the fog. Ray was completing his investigation of the incident when 100 Iraqis walked out of the fog and surrendered. When Marines around the 1st Marine Division's HQ began hearing the rumble of armored vehicles beyond the front, Captain Ray knew something was wrong. As the fog and smoke from the oil fires began to lift, an Iraqi mechanized division clashed with Company C, 1st Battalion, 1st Marines and the LAV crews of Company B and Task Force Shepherd. The fight lasted nearly an hour before the Iraqis withdrew. After reorganizing, the enemy attempted a second push, but were greeted by Marine AH-1W Super Cobras. The final attack came at 1100hrs and ended dramatically for the enemy, with a loss of 27 APCs and two tanks and more than 300 infantry personnel captured. Captain Ray, who prior to the battle wanted desperately to get his company into the fight, had the fight literally drive into his position. For his leadership and calm under fire Ray was awarded the Navy Cross. He was one of only two Marines to receive the Navy Cross during the conflict.

Captain Eddie S. Ray – Navy Cross Citation
Captain Eddie S. Ray, United States Marine Corps, for extraordinary heroism while serving as CO, Company B, First Light Armored Infantry Battalion, Task Force Shepherd, FIRST Marine Division, in the Emirate of Kuwait on 25 February 1991. During the early morning hours of G+1 of Operation Desert Storm, an Iraqi mechanized division counter-attacked elements of the FIRST Marine Division in the vicinity west of the flame and smoke engulfed Burgan Oil Fields in Southeastern Kuwait. As dense black smoke shrouded the battlefield, an Iraqi mechanized brigade engaged the FIRST Marine Division Forward Command Post security forces. During the ensuing intense ten hour battle, Captain Ray repeatedly maneuvered his Light Armored Vehicle Company in harm's way, skillfully integrating his Light Armored Infantry weapons, reinforcing TOWs, and AH-1W Attack Helicopters to decisively defeat main Iraqi counter-attacks. Leading from the front and constantly exposed to large volumes of enemy fire, Captain Ray led swift, violent attacks directly into the face of the vastly larger enemy force. These attacks shocked the enemy, destroyed 50 enemy Armored Personnel Carriers, and resulted in the capture of over 250 Iraqi soldiers. Operating perilously close to the attacking enemy, Captain Ray's courage, composure under fire, and aggressive war fighting spirit were instrumental in the defeat of a major enemy effort and the successful defense of the Division Forward Command Post. By his outstanding display of decisive leadership, unlimited courage in the face of heavy enemy fire, and utmost devotion to duty, Captain Ray reflected great credit upon himself and upheld the highest traditions of the Marine Corps and the United States Naval Service.

The final push

As Task Force Shepherd's Marines drove through the Al Burqan oilfields towards Phase Line Margaret (the designated staging area before the division's final push to cut off Kuwait International Airport), the force continued to screen for the division. En route to Phase Line Margaret, Company C knocked out ten Type 63 APCs, while Company A followed, destroying six more APCs and capturing multiple enemy vehicles at an Iraqi supply point.

After leaving Phase Line Margaret, the LAVs of Task Force Shepherd continued screening for the division. During their subsequent advance, the Marines of the task force destroyed six tanks, 11 APCs, and five trucks before reaching the perimeter fence of the airport. The task force headed north to the city racetrack, where they came across Kuwaiti resistance members, who informed them that most of the Iraqis had fled the city. The LAVs of Task Force Shepherd had reached Phase Line Green, the preplanned limit of the division's advance. General Myatt ceased all offensive operations at 0647hrs on February 28, 1991.

The end of combat operations, however, did not terminate the presence of Marine LAVs operating within theater. The 2nd LAI Battalion provided detachments in support of Operation *Provide Comfort*; the detachments were assigned to the 24th and 26th Marine Expeditionary Units (MEUs) from April 1991 through January 1992.

Operation *Uphold Democracy*

In September 1991, the President of Haiti, Jean Bertrand Aristide, was overthrown by elements of the Haitian military. United Nations (UN) efforts to restore power to President Aristide, who was freely elected, failed. Three *de facto* government regimes later and the country had experienced extreme repression, including government-sanctioned torture, assassinations, and rape. By 1994 the UN adopted Resolution 940. The resolution authorized member states of the UN to utilize "all necessary means" to restore the situation in Haiti.

The Marines of Company B, 2nd LAI Battalion, from Camp Lejeune were deployed to Haiti in support of Operation *Uphold Democracy*. The need for LAVs was two-fold. First the vehicles could add additional transportation resources in the possible evacuation of all US citizens from Haiti. Second, memories of a costly raid by US Army Rangers and Delta Force in Somalia in October 1993 were still burned into the minds of the planners. These elite soldiers had no light armor at their disposal, and took heavy casualties during the fighting in the streets of Mogadishu.

The Special Purpose Marine Air-Ground Task Force (SPMAGTF), with a force of more than 1,900 Marines, was tasked with restoring order in Haiti. The Marines of Company B were staged and ready for the planned September 19 landings into Cap-Haitien, in support of Battalion Landing Team (BLT) 2/2. The LAV crews made up part of Task Force Irish. The task force would come ashore utilizing Landing Craft, Air Cushion (LCAC) and Utility Landing Craft (ULC) and seize the town by force. A second task force, Task Force Hawg, would use vertical envelopment in order to take the town's airport. Just before H-Hour, the invasion was called off by a diplomatic mission led by former President Jimmy Carter. While the landings would now occur with different rules of engagement, much of the initial landing plans stayed the same.

Company B's LAVs came ashore with live ammunition at the ready and buttoned up. Large crowds of civilians greeted the Marine crews, applauding their presence. The Haitian armed forces were not as thrilled, and used intimidation and brutality to cool the crowd's enthusiasm for the newly arrived US forces. The LAV-25's speed and versatility were used to great effect in securing Cap-Haitien. Using concertina wire stowed on their vehicles, the crews set up security checkpoints within minutes. The LAVs and Amphibious Assault Vehicles (AAVs) of Task Force Irish had a psychological effect on the abusive members of the Haitian armed forces and police force. The sheer physical presence of these vehicles intimidated many Haitian resisters. The civilian populace also understood this, and cheered the crews as they drove by. Marine LAV crews of Task Force Irish were called upon to aid in convoy escort, the seizure of weapons, disarming Haitian forces, and providing assistance at the various relief distribution points. In the classic Marine role, once the situation on the ground was stabilized, the Marines of SPMAGTF turned over operations to the US Army counterparts and redeployed back to Camp Lejeune. Marine LAV crews revisited Haiti in 2003–04 to help stabilize the region and again in January 2010 during Operation *Unified Response* after a 7.0-strength earthquake devastated Port au Prince.

Peace Enforcers

The LAV's true strength is its versatility to adapt to a variety of missions. Traditionally, missions involving urban environments prove especially challenging for armored crews to operate within. Patrolling street by street restricts the LAV-25's greatest characteristics, its speed and maneuverability. Throughout the LAV-25's history, however, it has operated as a peace enforcer, confronted with operating within these parameters.

One of the more unique missions in the vehicle's history involved the 1992 Los Angeles Riots. The riots started on April 29 following the acquittal of four white police officers accused of beating African-American motorist Rodney King following a high-speed pursuit. After three days of rioting in the city, state officials requested federal assistance. On May 1, elements of the 1st LAI Battalion stationed at Camp Pendleton deployed to Los Angeles to assist civilian authorities curb widespread looting. Marines of the 1st LAI assisted the Long Beach Police department with patrols aimed at quelling the crowds. The federal intervention utilizing the Marines and National Guard soldiers from Fort Ord helped stabilize the situation.

Marine LAV-25 crews from the 2nd LAR Battalion pass through the town of Koretin, Kosovo, greeted by local citizens, June 1999. (DoD)

Operation *Restore Hope*

In 1992, widespread famine in Somalia killed more than half a million people. International relief efforts to help the population had been hampered by clan violence. With thousands of people dying of starvation, President George H.W. Bush deployed thousands of US service members to the affected area during Operation *Restore Hope*. The multinational force, led by US troops, was charged with ensuring that humanitarian aid could reach the affected people.

On December 9, 1992, Marines assigned to the 15th (MEU) Special Operations Capable (SOC) made their initial landings into Mogadishu, Somalia. A light armored infantry platoon from the 3rd LAI helped reinforce the 2nd Battalion, 9th Marines, who were the main body of the ground combat element (GCE). Marines came ashore at 0540hrs and were greeted by the bright lights of television cameras from news crews covering the landing. The Marines quickly pushed through the media obstruction and pressed to secure the port facility and airport. They were able to secure their initial objectives and advanced through the streets of Mogadishu to the US embassy compound. The embassy became the headquarters for the joint Unified Task Force (UNITAF) Somalia.

On December 15, a joint operation consisting of Marines from the 15th MEU and French forces launched a successful campaign to secure the city of Baidoa, known as the "City of Death" due to the excessive famine and its suffering at the hands of the warring factions. The LAV crews that participated in securing Baidoa helped provide security for convoy after convoy of urgent relief supplies.

Advanced elements of the 3rd LAI Battalion arrived in Mogadishu on December 19. With Baidoa secured, the UNITAF staff pushed to secure another city in ruins, Bardera. The 3rd LAI had been in-theater only a few days when called into action. It worked in conjunction with AAVs from the 3rd Amphibious Assault Battalion to support the 7th Marines push toward the city. After a long road march, the Marines secured Bardera airfield, and by Christmas all access to the city was controlled and patrols began controlling the city. Soon relief supplies started to reach the beleaguered population.

E OPERATIONS IN KOSOVO (1999) AND IRAQ (2005)

1: A Marine Corps LAV-AT operating in Karabilah, Iraq, during Operation *Iraqi Freedom*, June 18, 2005. With its advanced optics suite and the heavy weaponry associated with the Emerson turret, the antitank variant is often utilized as a lead element, giving the battalion more advanced warning and greater firepower than an LAV-25. An LAV-AT crew consists of four members: a driver, commander, gunner, and loader. The vehicle carries a total of 16 TOW missiles, two within the turret and 14 stowed within the hull of the vehicle. The gunner's hatch is left slightly open and the loader's hatches are in the open position for quick reloading of the turret. The Marine LAV crews are participating in Operation *Spear*, an action aimed at disrupting and rooting out foreign insurgent activities in the area.

2: An LAV-25 from the 2nd LAR Battalion is seen here prior to an upcoming mounted patrol through the village of Zerga, Kosovo, June 1999. Marines from 2nd LAR were assigned to the 26th MEU while participating in Operation *Allied Force*. This particular vehicle had the name "LAND SHARK" painted on the side of the turret. Forward of the vehicle's name is a large ammunition box used to stow additional gear along with the vehicle commander's binocular case. Both the gunner's and commander's 782 gear (personal gear) are stowed behind their hatches. The NATO acronym KFOR (which stands for Kosovo Force) was hastily painted in white on all four sides of the hull to help identify the vehicle as friendly for ground forces; the LAV also wears a bright orange VS17 signal panel placed on the back of the turret to aid identification by coalition aircraft.

1

2

On January 6, 1993, members of General Mohamed Farah Hassan Aideed's Somali faction fired on a Marine convoy driving through Mogadishu near two authorized weapons storage sites. Marine Forces Somalia responded with an overwhelming demonstration of power, and created Task Force Mogadishu. The task force had firepower from a variety of weapon systems: AH-1W Super Cobras, UH-1N Iroquois helicopters, plus M1A1 Abrams Tanks, AAVs, and LAV-25s, all in support of the Marines on the ground. The attack plan had LAV crews from the 3rd LAI establish a screen line while the infantry surrounded the two weapons storage facilities, with sniper support observing the target area. By 2300hrs on January 7, the two Marine rifle companies had both facilities surrounded. Marines reported seeing Somali fighters preparing a tank and an antiaircraft gun. Snipers eliminated the antiaircraft machine-gun crew, opening a general firefight. At 0615hrs, Marine AH-1Ws were cleared hot and brought in to suppress remaining enemy combatants. At 0647hrs, Marine M1A1 tanks followed by Marines of Company K (who had four LAVs attached) were within the compound. Fighting stopped at 0926hrs. In one of the largest firefights during Operation *Restore Hope*, Marines captured four M47 Patton Tanks, 13 APCs, and various field/air defense artillery. Members of General Aideed's faction failed to inflict any casualties and were humiliated by the engagement.

Marine LAV crews from the 2nd and 3rd LAI would continue to play an integral part in the humanitarian/peacekeeping mission, performing a variety of missions from convoy escort, security patrols, to establishing security checkpoints. By May 1993, the redeployment of Marine Forces was completed following a planned change of responsibility from UNITAF forces to UN troops. A platoon from the 3rd LAR Battalion (re-designated on March 1, 1994) would return to Somalia in 1995 for Operation *Unified Shield*.

Operation *Joint Guardian*
Marine LAV crews from Company D (Reinforced) assigned to the 26th MEU supported BLT 3/8 as the force drove into Kosovo from Macedonia on June 14, 1999. The company had eight LAV-25s organized into two platoons and an LAV-M mortar section with two vehicles. The Marines had additional firepower in the form of three TOW-mounted HMMWVs integrated within the company. The headquarters and logistics element deployed with one LAV-C2, one LAV-R, one LAV-L, and a single HMMWV. The crews were deployed to enforce the tenets of the military technical agreement between NATO forces and the Yugoslavian Army.

During the early stages of this deployment, the LAV crews were used for traditional route, area, and zone reconnaissance missions throughout the entire Marine sector. Information gathered by the crews helped determine which towns and villages needed a permanent presence of force. The reconnaissance missions also helped keep track of the Serbian forces' withdrawal from the embattled country. Typically, towns with a high mix of Albanian and Serbian populations were the most dangerous. Within the Marine sector, the city of Gnjilane was one of the most heated. Company D utilized "presence patrols" to monitor the situation within the city. Patrols consisted of one LAV-25 platoon (four LAV-25s) with either a single logistics or recovery vehicle and a TOW-mounted HMMWV. A second platoon waited in reserve as a quick reaction force if needed. The patrols operated day and night with the platoons switching roles. The make-up of the reinforced platoon ensured the Marines had all the necessities to operate independently.

An LAV-25A2 crew conducts a weapons sighting mission in Helmand Province, Afghanistan. The commander and gunner stand under some makeshift shade created from camouflage netting. The view offers a close look at the LAV-25A2's weapon systems. A pair of 7.62mm ammo cans sit below the commander's M240 pintle-mounted machine gun. (DoD)

Due to their powerful sights the TOW HMMWVs attached to the patrols were utilized in an overwatch capacity. The vehicles observed the town or village from a distance before and during the patrol. Once inside the town, where the line platoons' vision was limited, the patrols counted on the TOW HMMWVs for threat information. The LAV crews from Company D ended their highly successful peacekeeping operations in July 1999.

Operation *Enduring Freedom*

On September 11, 2001, the World Trade Center in New York and the Pentagon in Washington DC were attacked by Al Qaeda terrorists. On November 25, 2001, Marines began combat operations to deprive Al Qaeda of their base of operations within Afghanistan.

Assigned to the 15th MEU (SOC), a detachment from Company B of the 1st LAI Battalion deployed to Afghanistan in December. The Marines conducted a variety of missions, operating through the rugged terrain near Kandahar. In January 2002, a platoon from Alpha Company also went to Afghanistan in support of the 3rd Battalion, 6th Marines BLT assigned to the 26th MEU. The Marines again operated within Kandahar Province and conducted numerous reconnaissance missions and mounted patrols, as well as established vehicle and human traffic control points. In October 2008, Marine LAV crews from Company B, 2nd LAR, began operations within Helmand Province. The platoon-sized element conducted patrols and reconnaissance missions in support of the 1st Battalion, 6th Marines, assigned to the 24th MEU. Members of 2nd LAR continued to operate within Helmand Province throughout 2008; during their deployment the Marines established two combat outposts and several law enforcement stations for the Afghan National Police and Border Patrol.

Operation *Iraqi Freedom*

Elements of all four LAR battalions within the Marine Corps participated in the 1st Marine Division's drive into Iraq during Operation *Iraqi Freedom*. The

Two Afghan interpreters ride along with a Marine LAV-25 crew from the 26th MEU conducting a mounted patrol near Kandahar International Airport, Afghanistan, January 17, 2002. (DoD)

1st LAR Battalion deployed to Kuwait in January 2003, and the 3rd LARB deployed its companies in January through February. The 3rd LARB arrived minus Company C, and it attached a reserve company from 4th LARB before combat commenced. Companies from 2nd LARB arrived in Kuwait in early February. Elements of the 4th LAR Battalion would deploy to Iraq in April as follow-on forces. The 1st, 2nd, and 3rd LAR Battalions were assigned to various regimental combat teams in preparation for the upcoming invasion.

Organizational Table (*Iraqi Freedom* – Initial Drive, March 2003)

Regimental Combat Team-1	2nd LAR Battalion
Regimental Combat Team-5	1st LAR Battalion
Regimental Combat Team-7	3rd LAR Battalion (Reinforced)
(2nd MEB) Task Force Tarawa	Company C, 2nd LAR Battalion

The march to Baghdad

On March 20, 2003, companies from the 1st and 2nd LAR Battalions crossed the Kuwaiti border into Iraq and started their lightning attacks towards the north. The 3rd LAR Battalion followed on March 21. As the brute power of the 1st Marine Division (Reinforced) headed north, Marines from Task Force Tarawa were tasked to secure key bridges crossing the Euphrates River within An Nasiriyah. The coalition's plans to drive north needed these bridges intact.

COYOTE PATROL, AFGHANISTAN (2007)

Coyote reconnaissance vehicles from Alpha Squadron, 3 R22R Battle Group protect a convoy made up of British and Canadian troops from the Royal Gurkha Regiment and the Operational Mentoring and Liaison Program (OMLP), November 22, 2007. The Canadian Coyote crews scan their sectors of fire during a brief stop, and offset their turrets to provide 360-degree observation. The convoy covered more than 110 miles of dangerous roads before reaching their final destination, the capital city of Oruzgan Province, Tarin Kowt. The lead vehicle's turret is covered in additional gear. Plastic water bottles can be seen taped upside down to the antenna masts of the vehicles; chemical lights are placed in the water bottles at night to help identify the vehicle's unit. Towards the front of the vehicle is a menacing row of star-shaped tire cutters, deployed in conjunction with concertina wire. The cutters help stop vehicles from overrunning the Coyote's position at checkpoints and roadblocks. The Canadian Coyote also incorporates a large metal frame to stow a spare tire on the front of the vehicle. Unlike US and Australian versions of the LAV-25, the Coyote has no trim vane for amphibious operations

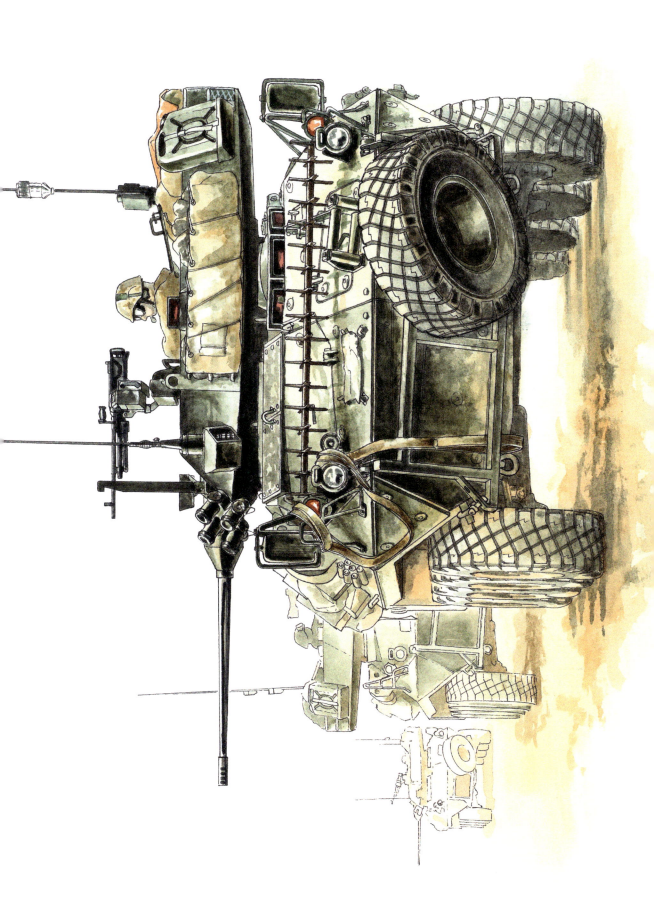

Secondary explosions erupt after Marine LAV crews from Delta Company, 1st LAR Battalion, destroy an enemy ammunition supply building during a firefight with Iraqi forces, April 5, 2003. (DoD)

Crews from the 2nd LAR Battalion fought small Iraqi detachments during the maneuver. Just after setting up a defensive position north of An Nasiryah, the unit faced one of its toughest fights. The battalion's defensive positions straddled Highway 7, and soon after positioning their vehicles in a defensive formation they were attacked by Iraqi forces utilizing direct and indirect fire. The Marines repelled the attack in a fight that would became known as "The Battle for the Coil." After this firefight and other engagements with the 2nd LAR Battalion, the enemy referred to the LAV-25s as "Destroyers," a name 2nd LARB adopted.

On March 23, heavy fighting took place in An Nasiriyah itself. With the assistance of a company from 2nd LAR, US forces held the bridges intact. Later that evening, Marines of 3rd LAR were ordered to move even further north, near the town of Hantush. The Marines were well north of the 1st Marine Division and were met with a nasty surprise. Major Bruce Bell, a company commander from 3rd LAR, noted that, "The *Fedayeen* [Iraqi militia] had actually laid out a decent 'U'-shaped ambush spread over 500 meters on both sides of the road. They picked a tactically sound, defensively oriented bend in the highway to exploit massed surprise fires on the lead units of whoever fell into the trap." According to Bell, Marines faced a column of at least ten tanks, APCs, and other and other vehicles.

The Marines from 3rd LAR were caught in an intense firefight. Believing they would soon be overrun, they called for immediate air support. The 3rd Marine Air Wing (MAW) answered with AH-1W Cobras and AV-8B Harriers, breaking apart the ambush.

A day after the fierce combat in An Nasiriyah, the "Mother of all Sand Storms" hindered the coalition's efforts. The storm let up on March 26, but rain followed, creating thick mud. The drive continued north, however, with LAV crews from the 3rd LAR Battalion assisting Regimental Combat Team-5 (RCT-5) in securing Hantush Airfield. The drive halted for a short time in order to consolidate division supplies. During the pause, aircraft from the 3rd MAW continued their strikes, dismantling Iraqi units in preparation for the 1st Marine Division's drive north to Baghdad.

On April 1 the offensive pause was lifted, and LAV crews of the 1st Marine Division headed north with their respective RCTs towards Baghdad. On April 7, RCT-7 led the 1st Marine Divisions' RCTs across the Diyala River, on the outskirts of Baghdad. The division's size made the

An LAV-25 crew from the 3rd LAR Battalion, 1st Marine Division, look vigilantly at their surroundings while on a mounted patrol through the city of Ar Rutbah, Iraq, January 1, 2005. (DoD)

crossing difficult. Marines utilized assault bridges (set up by the 8th Engineer Support Battalion) and captured enemy bridges, and in some cases swam their vehicles across the river. As the Marines started their final assault on Baghdad they were not met with heavy resistance. Instead, to their surprise, they were greeted by jubilant crowds. A Fox News team embedded with an LAV crew from the 3rd LAR Battalion showed scores of cheering civilians, reminiscent of a scene from the liberation of Europe in World War II.

Task Force Tripoli
With Baghdad captured, I MEF issued a warning order to the LAV battalions, and planned to utilize the three reinforced LARBs in order to take the Kirkuk oil fields. The target was later changed to Saddam Hussein's home town of Tikrit, after Kurdish fighters seized Kirkuk with the assistance of US Army Special Forces teams.

On April 12, Task Force Tripoli headed north to Tikrit. While passing through the town of Samarra en route to their objective, the commander of Company D, 3rd LAR Battalion, Lieutenant Colonel Herman S. Clardy III, was given information on the whereabouts of multiple US prisoners of war (POWs) within the city. The information came from an Iraqi police officer, who later volunteered to use a GPS device to pinpoint their location. The LAV commander, on his own initiative, sent his dismounted scouts along with intelligence team members to free the POWs. Seven American captives were rescued without incident, and the story made national headlines. Five of the soldiers were from the 507th Maintenance Company ambushed in An Nasiriya. The two others were Apache helicopter pilots whose aircraft had been brought down by enemy fire. Here was the second time Marines had rescued soldiers from the US Army's ill-fated 507th Maintenance Company. On March 23,

Marines from the 2nd LAR Battalion conduct a patrol through the streets of Rawah, Iraq, within Al Anbar Province, March 2007. Assigned to the weapons platoon of Delta Company, the Marines move alongside their LAV-25, the vehicle providing cover for the dismounted patrol. A role of concertina wire hangs off the front of the vehicle and can be utilized to set up a hasty roadblock. (DoD)

when the 507th convoy was ambushed, Marines from Task Force Tarawa went in and rescued ten of the stranded soldiers, four of whom were wounded.

On the same day as the POW rescue, Task Force Tripoli fought its way into Tikrit. By April 15 fighting had ceased and control of the city belonged to the Marines. On April 21, well after combat operations had ceased, the US Army's 4th Infantry Division took over responsibility for Tikrit. Task Force Tripoli was later utilized in southern Iraq to conduct reconnaissance-in-force missions near the Iraq/Saudi border. Similar missions were carried out by Marines of the 4th LAR Battalion, who were tasked with conducting surveillance and reconnaissance along the border between Iraq and Iran. By the end of June 2003, most of the LAV battalions had redeployed back to their home stations.

The insurgency

Soon after major combat operations ended in Iraq, a new war began. Instead of a standing army, the enemy was now an ever-growing insurgency. The Marine Corps would once again deploy elements from the four LAR battalions to Iraq. Marine Corps operations would concentrate on Al Anbar Province, geographically the largest province in Iraq. Support and stability operations within cities like Fallujah, Haditha, Al Asad, Al Qaim, and Ramadi were no easy tasks. The battles that raged for control over the city of Fallujah alone made it a household name within the United States. With the toughest enemy being IED attacks, the Marine Corps looked at ways of creating upgrades within the LAV program to increase the vehicles' survivability from these types of attacks. The improvements that came about from the lessons learned would eventually create the LAV-A2.

LAV-25 IN BATTLE, IRAQ (2003)
A Marine LAV-25 engages Iraqi forces in northern Iraq during the early stages of Operation *Iraqi Freedom*, April 5, 2003. The scouts open up their hatches and cover the vehicle's flanks and rear with their M249 Squad Automatic Weapon (SAW) machine guns. One of the scouts plugs his ears as the vehicle commander and gunner engulf the Iraqi targets with both 25mm M242 Bushmaster chain-gun fire and 7.62mm M240 machine-gun fire. The large markings on the vehicles' rear hatches (D/1) indicate that this LAV-25 crew is from Delta Company, 1st LAR Battalion of the 1st Marine Division. The LAV-25 wears multiple bright orange signal panels on the sides and rear of the turret to identify the vehicle as friendly to aid allied aircraft.

Marines from the 2nd LAR Battalion guard a checkpoint in Fallujah, Iraq, in their LAV-25. The Marines find a chance to eat and relax while sitting in the shade provided by their vehicle. The box of Meals Ready to Eat (MREs) behind the vehicle still bears mud from being transported wedged above the propeller. (DoD)

CONCLUSION

From its first actions in Operation *Just Cause*, Panama, to operating in the unforgiving mountainous terrain of Afghanistan during Operation *Enduring Freedom*, the Light Armored Vehicle-25 has proven itself to be a versatile weapon system that continues to stand the test of time. With the current A2 upgrades, the light armored vehicle is scheduled to remain within the Marine Corps' inventory well into the 21st century. Perhaps the most astonishing fact concerning the LAV-25's success is that the program that began as an off-the-shelf procurement for the Marine Corps has become the foundation for multiple weapon systems, including the Australian ASLAV and the Canadian Coyote. After nearly thirty years of service and as a veteran of every major Marine combat action since its introduction, the LAV-25 family of vehicles has earned its place as one of the great combat weapon systems of the United States Marine Corps.

BIBLIOGRAPHY

Andrew Jr., Rod., *U.S. Marines in Battle An Nasiriyah,* History Division Headquarters USMC, Washington D.C. (2009)

Cureton, Charles H, *Marines in the Persian Gulf 1990–1991: With the I Marine Division in Desert Shield and Desert Storm,* History & Museum Division Headquarters USMC, Washington D.C. (1993)

An LAV-25A2 crew assigned to the 22nd MEU executes an amphibious assault landing from a US Navy Landing Craft, Utility (LCU). The Marines are taking part in Exercise *Bright Star* in Alexandria, Egypt, October 12, 2009. (DoD)

Hunnicutt, R.P., *Armored Car*, CA, Presidio (2002)

Jane's *Armour & Artillery*, 1983–2010 editions.

Kozlowski, Francis X., *U.S. Marines in Battle An Najaf*, History Division Headquarters USMC, Washington D.C. (2009)

Mauskapf, Robert P., Powers, Earl W. *LAVs in Action*, Marine Corps Gazette (Sep. 1990)

Michaels, G.J., *Tip of the Spear U.S. Marine Light Armor in the Gulf War* (2008)

Mrocakowski, Dennis P., *Marines in the Persian Gulf 1990–1991: With the II Marine Division in Desert Shield and Desert Storm*, History & Museum Division Headquarters USMC, Washington D.C. (1993)

Mrocakowski, Dennis P., *Restoring Hope in Somalia with the Unified Task Force 1992–1993*, History Division Headquarters USMC, Washington D.C. (2005)

Quilter II, Charles J., *Marines in the Persian Gulf 1990–1991: With the I Marine Expeditionary Force in Desert Shield and Desert Storm*, History & Museum Division Headquarters USMC, Washington D.C. (1993)

Reynolds, Nicholas E., *A Skillful Show of Strength – U.S. Marines in the Caribbean, 1991–1996*, History Division Headquarters USMC, Washington D.C. (2003).

Reynolds, Nicholas E., *Just Cause, Marine Operations in Panama, 1988–1990*, History & Museum Division Headquarters USMC, Washington D.C. (1996)

Reynolds, Nicholas E. *U.S. Marines In Iraq, 2003: Basrah, Baghdad And Beyond*, History Division Headquarters USMC, Washington D.C. (2007)

Tanzola, Robert L, Markiewicz, Jonathan A., Laing, Phillip C., *Light Armored Reconnaissance*, Marine Corps Gazette (Nov. 1999)

Unit Histories; and Lineage & Honors from, 1st Light Armored Reconnaissance Battalion, 2nd LAR Battalion, 3rd LAR Battalion, 4th LAR Battalion.

Westermyer, Paul W., *U.S. Marines in Battle Al Khafji 28 January – 1 February 1991*, History Division Headquarters USMC, Washington D.C. (2008)

INDEX

References to illustrations are shown in **bold**.

Afghanistan **15**, **20**, **22**, **39**, 39, **40**
Aideed, Gen Mohamed Farah Hassan, faction 31, 38
aircraft: Fairchild A-10 Thunderbolt II **26**, 30–31; Lockheed C-5 Galaxy **9**; Lockheed C-141B Starlifter **32**; Vought A-7 Corsair II 26 *see also* helicopters
Al Qaeda 39
Alvis Ltd 4
amphibious capability 9
An Nasiriyah, Iraq 42
Aristide, Jean Bertrand 34
armament 12–13; ammunition **29**; cannon, Cockerill 90mm 4, 23; cannon, GAU-12 Equalizer 25mm rotary 16, **17**; chain gun, M242 Bushmaster 25mm 4, **9**, **12**, 12, 15–16, **44**; gun, EX35 low-recoil 105mm 16–17; machine gun, 7.62mm 9, 12–13, **14**, 15, 18, **24**, 26, **44**; machine gun, M249 Squad Automatic Weapon (SAW) **44**; missile, Stinger 15, **16**, **17**; missile, TOW guided **14**, 30, 31; mortars **15**, **16**; rocket pod, Hydra 70mm 15, 16; smoke grenade launcher, M257 9, **13**, 14, 15, 18
armor, upgraded 18
Arraiján, Panama 24, 25
ASLAV-25 (Australian Light Armored Vehicle-25) **20**, 20, **22**, 22
Australian Army **20**, 20, **22**, 22

Baghdad 42–43
Baidoa, Somalia 36
Bardera, Somalia 36
Bell, Maj Bruce 42
Bush, George H.W. 26, 36

Cadillac Gage (*later* Cadillac Gage Textron) 4, 16–17
Camp Pendleton, CA, Infantry Training School 6, **12**
Canadian armed forces **22**, 22–23, **40**
carrying capacity 12
Carter, Jimmy 34
Clardy III, Lt Col Herman S. 44
"Coil, The Battle of the" 42
construction 8–9, **11**, 12
Cougar, GM of Canada **5**, 5
Coyote (LAV-25 Reconnaissance) **22**, 22–23, **23**, 40
crew and positions 9, 12

Decker Jr., Maj Gen O.C. 5
development 4–5

exercises: *Bright Star* **47**; *Cold Winter 87* 6; *Highland Thunder* **17**; *Marex* 9

Fallujah, Iraq 44, **45**
FMC Corporation 15
Foster-Miller Inc. 18
Fox News 43
"friendly fire" incidents **26**, 30–31, 32

Gaskins, Capt Gerald H. 25, 26
General Electric (later General Dynamics) 15, 16, 20
General Motors of Canada (later General Dynamics Land Systems-Canada) 4–5, 23
Gnjilane, Kosovo 38–39
Gurkha Regiment, Royal **40**

Haiti **14**, 34–35
Haitian armed forces 34, 35
helicopters: Bell AH-1W Super Cobra 31, 33, 38; Sikorsky CH-53E Super Stallion **6**
Hussein, Saddam 26

Iraq **19**, 20, 36, 39–40, **42**, 42–44, **43**, 44, **46**; insurgency in 44
Iraqi forces 26, 28, 33, 34, **42**, 42; offensive 2–32
Isaak, Cpl Garreth 25

King, Rodney 35
Kosovo 35, 36, 38–39
Kuwait 26, 28, 32–34, 40, 42; International Airport **13**, 26

La Chorrera, Panama 25–26
Landing Craft: Air Cushion (LCAC) **9**, 34; Utility (LCU) **47**
LAV-25 4, 6, **9**, **12**, 28, 32; "CROAKER" **30**; "GUNSLINGER" **31**; "HI-BODY" **6**; "LAND SHARK" **36**; LAR Bn, 1st **44**; LAR Bn, 2nd **9**, 24, **25**, 26, 35, 44, **46**; LAR Bn, 3rd **43**; MEU, 26th **40**; US Army **28**, **29**
LAV-25 Reconnaissance (Coyote) **22**, 22–23, **23**, 40
LAV-25A1 19, 20
LAV-25A2 **10**, **19**, 19–20, **20**, 39, 44, 46, **47**
LAV-105 16–17
LAV-A1 *see* LAV-25A1
LAV-A2 program 19–20 *see also* LAV-25A2
LAV-AD (Air Defense) 15–16, **17**
LAV-AG (Assault Gun) 16–17, 23
LAV-AT (Antitank) **5**, 14, **15**, 30, 31, 36; turret **15**
LAV-C2 (Command & Control) 5, 8, **14**, 14
LAV-L (Logistics) 5, **8**, **13**, 13
LAV-M (Mortar) 5, 15, **16**
LAV-R (Recovery) 5, 8, 13–14, **14**
Los Angeles Riots 35

Metric Systems 19
MEWSS (Mobile Electronic Warfare System) 17–18, **18**
Mogadishu, Somalia 32, 34, 36, 38
Myers, Lt Col Clifford O. 28, 29, 32

Navy Cross awards 33
Noriega, Manuel 23

operations *Desert Shield/Storm* **13**, **26**, 26, 28, 28–34, **29**, **30**; final push 34; Iraqi offensive 29-32; into Kuwait 32–34; OP-4 battle **26**, 29–32; OP-6 battle 31; organizational structure 28
operations, other: *Allied Force* 36; *Big Show* **24**, 26; *Defeat Al Qaeda* 20; *Enduring Freedom* 15, 39, 39, 40; *Iraqi Freedom* 36, 39–40, **42**, 42–44, **43**, 44, **46**; *Joint Guardian* 38–39; *Just Cause* 13, 14, 23, **24**, 25–26; *Nimrod Dancer* 24; *Provide Comfort* 34; *Restore Hope* 36, 38; *Rough Rider* 14, 25; *Slipper* 20; *Southern Scimitar* **18**; *Spear* 36; *Unified Response* 35; *Unified Shield* 38; *Uphold Democracy* **14**, 34–35; *Westward Ho* 24
origins 4–5

Panama, US invasion (1989) 13, 14, 23–26, **24**, **25**, 26
Panamanian Defence Forces (PDF) 14, 23, 24, 25, **26**, 26
peace enforcers 35
performance 9
Pollard, Capt Roger L. **29**, 30–31
powerplant 8–9
production 5, 18
Protzeller, Capt Thomas P. 31

Quantico, Camp Upshur **10**

Rapid Deployment Task Force (RDTF) 4
Ray, Capt Eddie S. 33

Saudi Arabia 26, 28; "The Berm" 28
Saudi Arabian National Guard (SANG) LAV-25 23
September 11, 2001, terrorist attacks 39
Service Life Extension Program (SLEP) 19
Ship, Maritime Prepositioning (MPS) 28
Shupp, Capt 31
Sight System, Raytheon AN/PAS-13 Improved Thermal (ITSS) 19–20
Somalia **31**, **32**, 34, 36, 38; Unified Task Force (UNITAF) 36, 38
specifications 9, **11**

tanks: M551 Sheridan 28, **29**, 29; T-55 29, 30, 31, 32; T-62 29, 31, 32
Tikrit, Iraq 44, 45
turret 8
Twentynine Palms, Marine Corps Air-Ground Combat Center 4, 5, 6

United Nations 34
upgrades **10**, 18–20 *see also* LAV-25A1; LAV-25A2
US Army 4, 5; Armored Regiment, 73rd, 3rd Battalion **28**, **29**; Maintenance Co., 507th 44–45
US Marine Corps 4, 5, 44
  changes within 5–6
  Company A (Reinforced) (later 3rd LAV Bn) 6, 8
  FAST (Fleet Anti-terrorist Security Team) 25, 26
  LAI (Light Armored Infantry) battalions (*later* LAR battalions) 6
  LAR (Light Armored Reconnaissance) battalions (*formerly* LAV & LAI battalions) 6
  LAR Battalion, 1st 8, **16**, **20**, 28, **29**, 35, 40; Company A 24, **25**, 26, 39; Company B 24, 34, 35, 39; Company C **30**, 33; Company D **20**, 24, 24–26, 39, **42**, 44; Company F **16**
  LAR Battalion, 2nd **8**, 9, 13, 14, 23, 24, 28, 32, 33, **35**, **36**, 38, 40, 42, **43**, 44, **46**; Company B 39
  LAR Battalion, 3rd 6, 8, **19**, 28, 36, 38, 40, 42, **43**, 43
  LAR Battalion, 4th **8**, **17**, 28, 40, 43; Company D **10**
  LAV (Light Armored Vehicle) battalions (*later* LAI & LAR battalions) 6
  Marine Air Wing, 3rd 42
  Marine Divisions: 1st 33, 39, 40, 42–43; 2nd **28**; 9th, 2nd Bn 36
  Marine Expeditionary Force, I (I MEF) 28, 44
  Marine Expeditionary Unit (MEU) 22nd **47**
  MEU, 26th **40**; Co. D (Reinforced) 38–39
  MEU SOC (Special Operations Capable), 15th 36, 39
  Operation *Desert Shield/Storm* organizational structure 28
  Recon Bn, 1st 29
  Regimental Combat Team-7 40, 42
  Special Purpose Marine Air-Ground Task Force (SPMAGTF) 34–35
  Task Force Hawg 34
  Task Force Irish 34, 35
  Task Force Ripper 32
  Task Force Shepherd **26**, 32, 33; Company A 31, 32, 33; Company B 32–33; Company C 31, 32, 33; Company D 29–32
  Task Force Tarawa **18**, 40, 44
  Task Force Tripoli 44–45
US prisoners of war 44

variants: export 20, 22–23; USMC 13–18 *see also individual entries*

Zerga, Kosovo 36